RIDBA

**Rural & Industrial
Design & Building Association**

Farm Buildings Handbook

2009 CANCELLED

Edited by

0 9 ard Langley CEng, MIAgrE, BSc(Hons) Agric Eng, MSc, Dip S, Cert Ed.

Published and Printed by Polstead Press
A The Maltings, Stowupland Road, Stowmarket, Suffolk IP14 5AG
Phone 01449 677444, Fax 01449 770028

Distributed by
Rural & Industrial Design & Building Association
5A The Maltings, Stowupland Road, Stowmarket, Suffolk IP14 5AG
Phone 01449 676049 Fax 01449 770028
Web site www.ridba.org.uk

Forward

This handbook has been produced as a ready reference point for farmers, designers and anyone else involved in the process of erecting a farm building. The book was originally published in its former guise by the Farm Buildings Association, when it was complied and edited by Sir Pat Astley Cooper, amongst others. I am pleased to see this completely new version of the handbook, brought back to print after a period of more than 17 years and expertly compiled by Richard Langley.

We have seen many changes in agriculture since the book was first published as the Farm Buildings Pocketbook. We have also seen many changes in the Farm Buildings Association, with two name changes. We now move forward as the Rural and Industrial Design and Building Association, encompassing all aspects of building in the countryside, but also acknowledging the fact that many of our members have as much, or more, involvement in industrial and commercial construction as they do in agricultural.

In common with the RIDBA, this handbook sets out to promote best practice for planning, designing and constructing farm buildings. Anybody following the advice contained within these pages will be well on their way towards constructing a sound and efficient building. Using competent, high quality designers, suppliers and contractors will ensure the conclusion of this process. RIDBA members are comitted to giving you this level of competence and quality.

I would like to thank our 2 sponsors Marley Eternit Ltd and the Training Fund of the Royal Agricultural Society of England, whose generous donations have allowed the project to go ahead and for this book to be sold at such a low price.

Jonathan Lace
RIDBA Chairman 2007 - 9

Acknowledgements

In re-writing and re-ordering this book, (last published pre-1992), I am indebted to the following people for their help, guidance and undoubted patience:

- Jim Loynes (Harper Adams University College)
- David Baldwin (Recogen Ltd)
- Charles Birch (Brown Co Ltd)
- David Wood (Agriquestrian)
- David Bishop (ICA Storage Ltd)
- Ian Barclay (Marley Eternit Ltd)
- Bill Leslie (Farm Electronics Ltd)
- Clive Mander - Editing Committee
- Jonathan Lace - Editing Committee
- Paul Grimshaw - Editing Committee
- Tony Hutchinson (RIDBA Secretary)
- Claire Edmonds (Harper Adams University College) for her professional typing skills

Disclaimer

Whilst every effort has been made to ensure the accuracy of the information included in this publication, the authors accept no responsibility in respect of this or any error or omission. Readers should satisfy themselves that they are complying with any variations in Legislation, rules or procedures relevant to their particular location or situation, prior to commencing work on any project. No endorsement of named products or manufacturers is intended and no adverse criticism is implied of similar products which are not mentioned.

Contents

Section 1

LEGISLATION AND REGULATIONS

1.1 Planning: A Do's and Don'ts summary

Do consider your ideas and options carefully; take time to prepare and plan your development proposals properly, and allow sufficient time for the process as a whole.

Do consider what effects your proposal might have on local amenity, the landscape and the environment, and on local services such as roads.

Do talk to your local planning authority - usually your local council - about your proposals; check whether you need planning permission and, if so, what local planning policies might be relevant to your proposals.

Do consult any neighbours or others who may be affected by your proposals, and your elected local councillor(s).

Do consider whether you might need professional advice and assistance (eg from planning consultants, land agents, surveyors) to prepare your planning application, particularly if your proposals involve large-scale or complex building development.

Do find out whether you are eligible for free planning consultancy advice under the Rural Enterprise Scheme administered by the Department for Environment, Food and Rural Affairs (DEFRA).

Do take account of all the advice and comments you receive, be prepared to amend your original ideas if necessary, and try to frame your proposals to bring out the positive impact they will have(eg improving the appearance of a run-down building, providing new employment opportunities, or facilities for the local community).

Do ensure that you present a clear and accurate planning application with supporting plans, covering all the points likely to be of concern to the planning authority.

Do respond positively and helpfully to any requests from the planning authority for further information; be prepared to be flexible in adapting your proposals to meet any concerns of the authority.

If your planning application is refused, do try to discuss the proposals with the planning officer to see if the planning authority's concerns can be overcome, before you consider whether to appeal.

Do read any guidance provided by your local planning authority.

Don't rush ahead with ill-considered and poorly prepared proposals.
Don't place too much weight on advice (eg from family or friends) about how to obtain planning permission unless it is confirmed by the planning authority or professional sources.

Don't rely on hearsay or assumptions (eg 'a neighbour has planning permission for a similar development, therefore I should get permission for my proposal').

Don't expect your local planning authority to tell you what sort of development (eg diversification) would be best for you - that is not their role - although you can ask the authority what type of developments are more likely to be acceptable in planning terms.

Don't assume that any indication of your chances of obtaining planning permission, that a planning officer might be prepared to give you prior to the submission of an application, will automatically be reflected in the final decision by the planning authority.

Don't expect an instant decision - you should allow at least eight weeks from the submission of your planning application, unless the planning authority has indicated otherwise.

Don't proceed with any development works without first checking with your local authority about the need for planning permission (or any other forms of consent), and until any necessary permission and other consents have been given.

Important note: Please note that Planning Laws and other Legislation may, and does, vary between England, Scotland, Wales and Northern Ireland. It has not been possible to include all these variations in this document. Therefore, readers should ensure that they are fully aware of any local variations, before starting a project.

1.2   Planning permission summary chart (Figure 1)

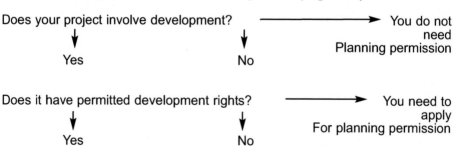

Check if you need the planning authority's approval for some details.

1.3 Do you need planning permission?

You do not always need planning permission. It is not required for agricultural operations or the use of existing buildings on agricultural land for agricultural purposes. It is also not required, generally speaking, for changes to the inside of buildings, or for small alterations to the outside (eg the installation of an alarm box). Permitted development rights exist for erecting (on holdings of 5ha or more), extending or altering a building, and for excavations and engineering operations, which are reasonably necessary for the purposes of agriculture within the unit. For most other types of development and change of use you will generally need to apply for planning permission.

1.4 Permitted development

The Town and Country Planning (General Permitted Development) Order 1995 (as amended) - the GPDO - provides a general planning permission (known as 'permitted development rights') for certain types of minor developments. The types of permitted development most likely to benefit farmers include:

- Temporary uses of land
- Agricultural buildings below a certain size
- Forestry buildings and forestry roads
- Caravan sites and related buildings in some circumstances

Permitted development rights are not available for farm or forestry dwellings, or for livestock units near residential and similar buildings.

Before making use of some agricultural permitted development rights, you should check if the local planning authority require their prior approval for certain details of the proposed development. In the case of agricultural building this will cover its siting, design and external appearance.

1.5 Environmental impact assessment

Environmental Impact Assessment (EIA) is a formal procedure under statutory regulations for ensuring that the potential effects on the environment of certain new development and land use change are fully considered before the development, or change, is allowed to go ahead. Under the *Town and Country Planning (Environmental Impact Assessment) (England and Wales) Regulations 1999*, the local planning authority considers the environmental effects of a proposed development, usually in reaching a decision on a planning application. EIA will not normally be required for most small scale development. EIA is mandatory for certain developments, such as installations for the intensive rearing of poultry (with more than 85, 000 places for broilers or 60, 000 places for hens), or pigs (with more than 3, 000 places for production pigs (over 30kg) or 900 places for sows). Similar intensive livestock installations and fish farming installations normally require EIA only if they are likely to have significant environmental effects. The planning authority will advise you if EIA is required.

(This should not be confused with the **Integrated Pollution Prevention and Control Permi**t - IPPC - which applies to pig and poultry farms with a capacity for more than:

- 40, 000 places for poultry (includes chickens, layers, pullets, turkeys, ducks and guinea fowl)
- 750 sows
- 2, 000 finishing pigs over 30kg

Existing farms need a permit if they are doing any of the following:

- Bringing into use a new farm that exceeds the thresholds
- Expanding a unit currently below the thresholds to above the thresholds
- Making a 'substantial change' to a farm already above the thresholds. (SAC, 04/06)).

1.6 Agricultural dwellings

Planning permission is always required for dwellings. In the open countryside away from existing settlements, or areas designated for development, planning permission is normally granted only in exceptional circumstances. For example, if it is essential for a farm worker to live at or in the immediate vicinity of the workplace in order to attend to livestock. If permission is granted in such circumstances, it is usually conditional on the dwelling being kept available to meet that agricultural need. Occupancy will therefore be restricted to people solely or mainly working in the locality in agriculture.

1.7 Preparing the ground before you apply

Step 1 - Contact your local planning authority, often available online Tell them what you want to do and ask about relevant local planning policies in the development plan and any special land designations that might apply. Ask if the authority foresees any difficulties with what you propose and how you should resolve them. If you would find it helpful, ask to meet a planning officer for an informal discussion; ask whether a formal Environmental Impact Assessment might be required.

Step 2 - If you think you may need professional advice and assistance, consider appointing an agent.

Step 3 - Consider what effects your proposal would have on local amenity, the environment and services.

Step 4 - Consult any neighbours and others who might be affected by your proposals, and your elected local councillors. If appropriate, consult other regulatory bodies.

Step 5 - Consider all the comments and advice you have received. If you intend to go ahead, consider whether you might amend your proposals to improve the chances of obtaining planning permission.

1.8 Making your application

Step 1 - Obtain an application form and any guidance notes from your local planning authority. Find out how many copies you will be required to submit. Normally three copies will be required.

Step 2 - Decide whether to apply yourself or appoint an agent to apply on your behalf.

Step 3 - Decide whether to apply for outline or full planning permission.

Step 4 - Complete the form, location and layout plans and illustrations.

Step 5 - Attach any additional information.

Step 6 - Send to the local planning authority with certificate of ownership or notification, and the correct fee.

Step 7 - Find out from the authority whether (and when) your application is likely to go before the planning committee, or if it will be delegated to planning officers to decide. Ask when a decision is likely to be made.

1.9 Outline planning permission

The more information you can give the better, but there is no need to submit detailed plans. If outline planning permission is given, you will then have to apply for approval of the details, which are known as 'reserved matters', before work can start. These comprise siting, design, external appearance, means of access and landscaping. What you propose must be consistent with the outline permission, or else you may need to reapply. This two-tier process takes longer than applying for full planning permission at the outset and there are two sets of fees. It does, however, have the advantage that time and money are not wasted on the detail of a proposal which is unlikely to be granted planning permission.

1.10 Full planning permission

Here you submit the necessary details to enable the planning authority to reach a decision. You will have to follow this course if you wish to change the use of property, whether land or buildings, or if you have carried out development without the necessary permission and want to make it lawful.

1.11 After the application

Step 1 - The local planning authority publicises your application.

Step 2 - The planning authority consults other bodies.

Step 3 - The planning authority considers any views and comments received.

Step 4 - The planning authority may contact you to discuss possible amendments to your application to meet any problems or objections.

Step 5 - A report is prepared for the authority's Planning Committee (you are entitled to attend the council meeting deciding your application) or the senior planning officer taking the decision.

Step 6 - You are informed in writing of the decision.

1.12 Refusal and right to appeal

Step 1 - If your planning application is refused, talk to the local authority planning officers to see if an amended proposal might succeed.

Step 2 - If appropriate, amend your application and re-apply for planning permission. Otherwise, consider whether you wish to appeal to the First Secretary of State.

Step 3 - Consider whether you need professional advice and assistance.

Step 4 - Submit your appeal within six months.

Step 5 - Await notification of the appeal decision.

1.13 Permitted development rights

The *Town and Country Planning (General Permitted Development) Order 1995* grants a general planning permission (known as 'permitted development rights') for certain types of development. Specific planning permission is NOT needed for:

- The use of land (but not any buildings) for any purpose (other than a caravan site) for not more than twenty-eight days in a year. However, for motor cycle or car racing, and markets (including car boot sales), only fourteen days a year are permitted. In Sites of Special Scientific Interest there are no permitted development rights for temporary uses of land for war games, clay pigeon shooting or any motor sports.

- Building, excavation or engineering operations designed for agricultural purposes (including those in connection with fish farming) on agricultural land in an agricultural unit of **5 hectares or more** which are reasonably necessary for the purposes of agriculture within the unit, provided that:

  o The development is not carried out on a separate parcel of land less than 1 hectare in area forming part of the unit
  o The development does not exceed 465m2
  o The building or structure is not higher than 12m, or 3m if within 3km of the perimeter of an aerodrome
  o The development is more than 25m from a trunk or classified road
  o The development does not involve the erection, extension or alteration of a dwelling
  o If the building is within 400m of the cartilage of a 'protected building', it is not to be used for the accommodation of livestock or for the storage of slurry or sewage sludge. ('Protected building' means a permanent building normally occupied by people, but does not include buildings within the agricultural unit, or any dwelling or building in agricultural use on any other agricultural unit).
  o If you are erecting a new building, forming a private way, carrying out excavations or depositing waste material, or placing or assembling a tank in any waters, you have applied to your local planning authority for a determination as to whether its prior approval will be required for certain details.
  o If you are extending or altering a building, you have not previously extended the cubic capacity by more than 10%; if it is in a National Park you have applied to the local planning committee for determination; if it is located elsewhere, and the alteration is 'significant' you have applied to the local planning authority.
  o If the development involves the extraction of any mineral from the land, the mineral is not moved off the unit.
  o It does not involve bringing waste materials onto the land from elsewhere.
  o It does not involve excavation or engineering operations connected with fish farming in a National Park or certain adjoining areas.

- Certain limited types of development on agricultural land in an agricultural unit of **not less than 0.4ha but less than 5ha**, which are reasonably necessary for the purpose of agriculture in that unit.

- The winning and working on land held or occupied with land used for the purposes of agriculture of any minerals reasonably necessary for agricultural purposes, within the agricultural unit of which it forms part.

• The use of land (but not a building) as a caravan site in certain circumstances.

• The erection, extension or alteration of buildings (except dwellings), or the formation, alteration or maintenance of private ways, where reasonably necessary for forestry purposes.

• The erection, construction, maintenance, improvement or alteration of a gate, fence, wall or other means of enclosure, provided that the height does not exceed one metre, next to a highway, or two metres elsewhere.

• The recreational or instructional use of land, and the pitching of tents, by organisations such as the Scouts, etc. (DEFRA, 2002).

1.14 Buildings: health and safety

The health and safety of everyone in the workplace is protected by 'The Workplace (Health, Safety and Welfare) Regulations 1992' and covers basic health, safety and welfare issues that apply to most workplaces. The general requirements to meet these regulations are covered in the HSE's Workplace health, safety and welfare: a short guide for managers. Due to the nature of farming, there are a number of areas which DEFRA has produced guidance. These are:

• The workplace - the Health and Safety Executive (HSE) booklet 'Farmwise: Essential guide to health and safety in agriculture' covers all aspects of health and safety for on-farm workplaces, including buildings. As an employer, you should ensure that buildings are kept in good repair, making sure that floors are not overloaded, particularly in feed lofts or older buildings. Workshops should be kept tidy, with no tripping hazards and inspection pits should be equipped with accessible escape routes. Handrails should be provided on stairs and ramps where necessary, with safety hoops or rest stages on long vertical fixed ladders used regularly, for example on grain bins. Lighting should be adequate and suitable. Flickering fluorescent tubes should be replaced although natural light should be used if possible, but try to avoid glare. Good drainage and non-slip floors are vital for areas likely to be wet, such as in milking parlours or buildings used for vegetable washing.

• Confined spaces - areas such as grain silos, slurry pits and silage clamps can present particular risks, including asphyxiation, drowning or danger from gases. Working in a confined space should therefore be avoided where possible, for example by undertaking work outside where feasible. Where it is impossible to do this, you should ensure safe working practices are followed and appropriate arrangements are made for rescue in an emergency. Sealed moist grain tower silos should only be entered when absolutely essential. They should never be entered to clear bridged grain. When working in a grain store, dust levels must be kept to a minimum, as described in the leaflet 'Controlling Grain Dust on Farms'. Cases of permanent lung damage, death and injury have been reported after exposure to gases in poorly ventilated indoor silage clamps. All slurry tanks above and below ground, sumps, reception pits and spaces under slatted floors present a high risk from noxious gases. Buildings above slatted areas where slurry is stored must be adequately and properly ventilated. Forage towers can be particularly dangerous. Dangerous concentrations of gases can occur just above the silage within an hour of filling. Information on minimising risks is contained in the HSE information sheet 'Managing Confined Spaces on Farms'.

Construction - most building projects, including many carried out on farms, must abide by the 'Construction (Design and Management) Regulations (CDM) 2007'. The regulations apply to all non domestic building projects but there are extra responsibilities for those where construction work takes more than 30 days, or there is more than 500 person days of construction work (30 days site). Construction work covers the clearing of the site through the fitting out of the building.

• Steel framed buildings present a high risk of collapse during erection unless proper precautions are taken and such work should be properly planned using the information sheet 'Controlling the Risk of Steel-Framed Farm Buildings Collapsing During Erection'. It is therefore important that a competent contractor is used. Corporate members of RIDBA sign up to a Code of Practice that proves that they are competent a list of them can be found at www.ridba.org.uk

• The construction or conversion of buildings for storing pesticides must be secured against unauthorised access and meet strict standards. Further details of health and safety considerations are contained in the information sheet 'Guidance on Storing Pesticides'.

• Roofs - on many farms roofs are fragile and unable to support a person's weight. You must know whether a roof is fragile before work starts and if you do not know treat it as fragile until a competent person has proved otherwise.. Many tasks do not require direct access. Inspecting a roof can be done from a telescopic handler, using a purpose-made people carrier. If using farm equipment to access a roof, it must be ensured that the working platform is safe to work from. For details see 'Lifting Operations and Lifting Equipment Regulations' (LOLER). A risk assessment must be carried out before any roof work. Appropriate precautions and systems of work should be provided and implemented. Working platforms or staging, also known as crawling boards, must be properly arranged and meet the correct specifications. People unsuited to working at heights, including those who suffer from vertigo, should not be asked to do this type of work. Training is usually required to achieve competence in roof work. Training providers such as college or training groups can provide further information, but roof work is dangerous and so only skilled and competent roof workers should access a roof. The law requires that precautions are taken to prevent falls from roofs. The booklet 'Why Fall for It? Details ways of preventing falls in agriculture. Best practice is covered in the HSE information sheet 'Preventing Falls from Fragile Roofs in Agriculture'. The information sheet 'Safe Working on Glasshouse Roofs' describes best practice methods for the horticultural sector. (DEFRA website, 04/2008) Reference should also be made to *ACR[CP]001:2007 Rev 2 Recommended Practice for work on Profiled Sheeted Roofs* and *ACR[CP]002:2005 "Safe Working on Fragile Roofs"*, both can be downloaded from www.roofworkadvice.info

1.15 Noise regulations

The *Control of Noise at Work Regulations 2005* (the Noise Regulations) came into force for all industry sectors in Great Britain on 6 April 2006. They replace the Noise Regulations 1989. The aim of the Noise Regulations is to ensure that workers' hearing is protected from excessive noise at their place of work, which could cause them to lose their hearing and/or to suffer from tinnitus (permanent ringing in the ears).

The level at which employers must provide hearing protection and hearing protection zones is now 85 decibels (daily or weekly exposure), and the level at which employers must assess the risk to workers' health and provide them with information and training is now 80 decibels. There is also an exposure limit value of 87 decibels, taking into account of any reduction in exposure provided by hearing protection, above which workers must not be exposed. (HSE website, 04/2008).

1.16 Temperature regulations

The Workplace (Health, Safety and Welfare) Regulations 1992 lay down particular requirements for most aspects of the working environment. Regulation 7 of these regulations deals specifically with the temperature in indoor workplaces and states that: 'During working hours, the temperature in all workplaces inside buildings shall be reasonable'. However, the application of the regulation depends on the nature of the workplace ie a bakery, a cold store, an office, a warehouse.

The associated approved code of practice goes on to explain that the temperature in workrooms should provide reasonable comfort without the need for special clothing. Where such a temperature is impractical because of hot or cold processes, all reasonable steps should be taken to achieve a temperature which is close as possible to comfortable. 'Workroom' means a room where people normally work for more than short periods.
The temperature in workrooms should normally be at least 16°C unless much

of the work involves severe physical effort in which case the temperature should be at least 13°C. These temperatures may not, however, ensure reasonable comfort, depending on other factors such as air movement and relative humidity.

Where the temperature in a workroom would otherwise be uncomfortably high, for example because of hot processes or the design of the building, all reasonable steps should be taken to achieve a reasonably comfortable temperature, for example by:

- Insulating hot plants or pipes
- Providing air-cooling plant
- Shading windows
- Siting workstations away from places subject to radiant heat

Where a reasonably comfortable temperature cannot be achieved throughout a workroom, local cooling should be provided. In extremely hot weather fans and increased ventilation may be used instead of local cooling.

Where, despite the provision of local cooling, workers are exposed to temperatures which do not give reasonable comfort, suitable protective clothing and rest facilities should be provided. Where practical there should be systems of work (for example task rotation) to ensure that the length of time for which individual workers are exposed to uncomfortable temperatures is limited. (HSE website, 04/2008).

1.17 COSHH

The *Control of Substances Hazardous to Health Regulations 2002* (as amended) aims to control exposure to agricultural dusts and protect workers' health. Agricultural dusts include grain and plant dusts, fungal spores, animal dander, bacteria and endotoxins. These can all cause diseases such as asthma, bronchitis and farmers' lung. Grain dust has a workplace exposure limit (WEL) of 10mg/m³ (based on an 8-hour weighted average) but exposure needs to be kept as low as reasonably practical below this limit. Special attention is necessary in grain reception pits, drying, handling and storage facilities, feed preparation and mill and mix units and livestock buildings. Remedies may include:

- Outdoor siting
- Management of crops
- Water fluming
- Enclosures

Dust can be controlled by good ventilation, filtering and re-circulation, electrostatic systems and wet scrubbers. There are no exposure limits for the other hazardous dusts covered by the sheet, but as a general rule exposure should be kept as low as reasonably practicable. (HSE website, 04/2008).

1.18 Dirty water/slurry

(i) The *Control of Pollution (Silage, Slurry and Agricultural Fuel Oil) Regulations 1991 (amended 1997)* is currently in force, and was made under the Water Act 1989. ('Slurry and waste' are covered later on, under new legislation). The main provisions of the Regulations are:

1.18.1 Silage

○ New silos must have an impermeable base, with perimeter effluent channels leading to an effluent tank. This tank must be capable of holding at least 20 litres of effluent for each cubic metre of silo capacity up to 1500m³; 6.7 litres per m³ is required for additional silo capacity above 1500m³

○ The regulations permit silage making in wrapped or sealed bales provided the bales are not stored or opened within 10m of a watercourse. An impermeable base for the storage is not required.

○ The field heap method of silage making (where silage is stored with no impermeable base, perimeter effluent channels or effluent tank) will only be permitted on farms where the majority of silage has been made this way over the last 3 years. The field heap method is not permitted in Scotland.

1.18.2 Fuel oil

○ Where more than 1500 litres of fuel oil is stored on the farm, above ground tanks and drums must be surrounded by an impermeable bund wall. The bund must be able to contain a specified volume of oil, or oil and water, and this varies depending on whether fuel tanks or drums are used.

○ Fixed taps and valves on tanks must discharge downwards and valves must be locked shut when not in use.

○ Discharge pipes from tanks must be fitted with a nozzle which contains an automatic shut-off device. This pipe must be locked within the bunded area when not in use.

○ The regulations do not apply to separately-stored domestic fuel oils. (See later section on 'fuel storage' for more details).

• In general, all new facilities must be at least 10m from any watercourses and inland or coastal waters. They also require a 20-year durability life. The Environment Agency must be notified of new, substantially enlarged or substantially reconstructed facilities, at least 14 days before they are used. It is an offence not to notify. The penalty for failing to comply with the regulations is a fine of up to £2000 on summary conviction, or unlimited fine on indictment. (Environment Agency website, 25/11/2004)

(ii) *The Code of Good Agricultural Practice for the Protection of Water 1998* provides practical guidance to help farmers and growers avoid causing pollution. Good agricultural practice means a practice that minimises the risk of causing pollution while protecting natural resources and allowing economic agriculture to continue.

1.18.3 Dirty water

- Minimise the amount of dirty water produced. Look for ways of separating clean and dirty water. Provide sufficient storage and containment so that dirty water can be managed and controlled properly. Keep stores and irrigation equipment in good repair.
- Check irrigation systems regularly and make sure warning devices and automatic cut-offs are working.

1.18.4 Livestock housing

- Wherever possible, collect and transfer slurry every day to a suitable store.
- Where bedding is required, use enough to keep livestock clean and keep all manure as dry as possible. Manage drinking systems to avoid over flow and spillage.
- Keep concrete areas around buildings clean and free from any build-up of manure and slurry.

1.18.5 Silage effluent

- Minimise the amount produced by wilting grass to 25% dry matter. Provide sufficient storage and containment for silage effluent so that it can be managed and controlled properly. Do not allow effluent into watercourses where even small amounts can kill fish and other water life.

1.18.6 Sheep dip

- Manage sheep dipping very carefully to avoid spillages and other uncontrolled releases to the environment. All sheep dips are very toxic and extremely small amounts can kill fish and other water life. They can also pollute groundwater and water supplies. You must get a written authorisation from the Environment Agency to spread used dip to land.

1.18.7 Smoke pollution

- Minimise the need to burn waste materials by first reducing the use of materials wherever possible, then recycling materials where appropriate and, finally, by using alternative environmentally acceptable methods of disposal wherever possible. If burning in the open is the only practical method of disposal, do not burn plastics, rubber or other materials known to produce dark smoke.

1.18.8 Energy efficiency

- Seek opportunities to use energy more efficiently and to exploit non-fossil fuels as sources of energy. Improvements to energy efficiency will reduce carbon dioxide (a greenhouse gas) emissions and can reduce farm running costs. (DEFRA, 2003).

1.19 Mains Water

All contracts involving mains water installations are required to adhere to the *Water Supply (Water Fittings) Regulations 1999*, which includes a system of prior notification and inspection.

1.20 Compliance

Compliance with legislation, codes of practice and all relevant assurance schemes will be necessary. Quality standards are no longer an option as soon as any product is to be marketed under an assurance scheme. *Farm Product Assurance Schemes* cover most of the main produce areas and set wide ranging standards in which buildings and their fittings usually play a large part. Voluntary codes of practice are specified as minimum standards, whether it is for vermin proof stores or lying space for cows.

1.21 Construction quality

Agricultural buildings are one of the few structures exempt from Building Regulation control, provided they are sited at a distance of not less than one-and-a-half times its own height from any building containing sleeping accommodation, and is provided with a fire exit not more than 30 metres from any point within the building. This does mean that any enclosed building over 30m long, such as a grain store, must have a fire exit to gain exemption. Building Regulation compliance will be required though for farm buildings that are converted to alternative uses; there is discussion on this topic later on.

'BS5502' is a British Standard for farm construction to give guidance on its functional and constructional design. Its application is voluntary, unless it is specified either by the purchaser or as part of environmental or quality assurance control; it may also be a planning approval condition. Details required for each part of the code will be outlined later in this text under the relevant section.

BS5502, Part 22, relates to occupancy, predicted safe lifespan, type of activity it is intended for, and the construction material's safe stressing limitations, together with its general suitability for the purpose and use.

1.21.1 Table 1: BS5502 Part 22: Design Life Classification of Buildings

Class, with example	Minimum design life reflecting strength of components in years	Human occupancy in hours/day at population density (persons/50m2)	Minimum distance in metres from classified road or non-owned dwelling place
1. Workshop, vegetable processing shed	50 years	Unrestricted	Unrestricted
2. Most farm buildings	20 years	6h/day at maximum density of 2 persons/50m^2	10m
3. Cow cubicle shed	10 years	2h/day at 1 person/50m2	20m
4. Plastic envelope sheep house	Temporary	1h/day at 1 person/50m^2	30m

It is essential that the minimum structural requirement of Class 2 (20 year minimum life) should be specified for **all** buildings unless the occupancy rate requires Class 1.

All buildings and structures conforming to the BS should have a plate fixed in a prominent position showing their:
- Classification
- Manufacturer
- Year of construction
- Retaining ability (if applicable), including reference to the limitations on loading (level or superimposed)
- For silage, the gross mass limit of the compressing vehicle, with appropriate warnings

1.22 The Construction (Design Management) Regulations 2007 (CDM)

The regulations apply to all non domestic building projects but there are extra responsibilities for those where construction work takes more than 30 days, or there is more than 500 person days of construction work (30 day site). Construction work covers the clearing of the site through the fitting out of the building.

The responsibility of the Farmer as a Client

- Ensure that everyone appointed to work on the project is competent to carryout the tasks required of them.

20

- Be satisfied that those appointed will allocate adequate resources to health and safety
- Provide information about the site (e.g. power cables in the ground, restrictions to the site, asbestos or other dangers)
- Allow for sufficient time and resources
- Must not set unrealistic building programmes that jeopardise safety.
- Ensure that a health and safety plan has been prepared before work starts on site and that the designers and contractors comply with it.
- On 30 day sites appoint a CDM Coordinator before design starts

1.23 Managing Asbestos on Farms (Control of Asbestos Regulations 2006)

This regulation, in simple terms, says that by May 2004 the following should have occurred:

- The duty holder must survey all non-domestic buildings
- Find all the reasonably accessible asbestos containing materials (ACMs)
- Record their condition
- Write a management plan based on the risk associated with the ACMs
- Advise all involved of the management plan
- More information can be found at
  http://www.ridba.org.uk/advicenotes/Managing_asbestos_on_farms.pdf

1.23.1 Recognising Asbestos Containing Materials (ACM) on the farm:

It is sometimes difficult to tell the difference between an asbestos cement product and a low-density insulation board, but there are a few rules that can be followed. The ACM will be asbestos cement if:

- The product has been used as a roofing or cladding product, open to the weather.
- The product is in sheet form and has been used as animal pens, or in wet areas. Low-density products were not robust enough to be used for this purpose nor could they withstand wet conditions without breaking down.

1.23.2 Managing asbestos containing products

- ACMs which are sound, undamaged and not releasing fibres, should not be disturbed. Their condition should be monitored on a regular basis
- Where possible, damaged materials should be repaired and then protected as necessary, provided that the repair or sealing will be durable and not likely to be disturbed
- Removal should only be performed where repair is not possible or the material is likely to be disturbed
- More information can be found at www.aic.org.uk

1.24 Sites of Special Scientific Interest (SSSI)

These 'conserve and protect the best of our wildlife, geological and physiological heritage for the benefit of present and future generations'. (DEFRA, 2003a). These are covered in the *Wildlife and Countryside Act 1981*, as amended by the *Countryside and Rights of Way Act 2000*. Sites may be either *Biological or Geological*; notification can cover any 'land' within the area of the conservation body; SSSIs are not necessarily open to the public, nor are they necessarily owned by the Government. The owners and occupiers of SSSIs are required to consult the appropriate conservation body if they want to carry out activities on the land. For example, 'grazing' would require consultation, even on chalk grassland or heathland where grazing is an essential part of management. If a proposal activity would not affect the interest or is beneficial to it, the conservation body will issue a 'consent' allowing it to be carried out without further consultation. (Wikipedia, 05/2008).

1.25 Nitrate Vulnerable Zones Regulations 2008 (NVZs)

A total of 55% of England was designated as a NVZ in October 2002, but a recent review of the existing NVZs indicates that the coverage should be about 70% of England. (Statutory Instruments, 2008). Farmers located in the current NVZs are required to apply 'Action Programme' measures to reduce nitrate leaching, and therefore slurry and other wastes are covered here. There are several key aspects to the current Action Programme measures, some of the main ones being:

1. Limit inorganic nitrogen fertiliser application to crop requirements, after allowing fully for residues in the soil and other sources.

2. Limit organic manure applications to 170kg/ha of total nitrogen each year averaged over the area of the farm not in grass, and 250kg/ha of total nitrogen each year averaged over the area of grass on the farm.

3. Do not apply slurry, poultry manure or liquid digested sludge between September 1st and December 15th (grassland on sandy and shallow soils) or August 1st and December 31st (arable land on sandy and shallow soils), or October 1st and January 15th (all other soils). The storage capacity available for those animal manures which cannot be applied during the autumn closed period must be sufficient to cover these periods unless other environmentally means of disposal are available.

4. Keep adequate farm records of his calculations of storage capacity.

5. A farmer who spreads organic manure on his land must make a written risk assessment of potential nitrate pollution to water from the spreading.

6. Before an occupier spreads organic manure on land he must undertake a field inspection to consider the risk of nitrogen getting into surface water.

7. It is an offence to spread nitrogen fertiliser, either organic or manufactured, on land with a slope of more than 12° if, taking account of ground cover and rainfall, there is a significant risk of nitrogen getting into surface water.

8. No person shall spread organic manure using high trajectory, high pressure equipment.

9. Storage facilities for all organic manure with high available nitrogen must be for a period of 26 weeks (6 months) for pigs and poultry, 22 weeks (5 months) for cattle.

10. Solid manure must be stored:
- In the building in which the livestock are kept
- At a suitable, temporary field site (this must NOT be within 50m of a spring, well or borehole, or within 10m of surface water or a field drain; it must not be located in one place for more than 12 consecutive months; it must not be in the same place as an earlier one constructed within the last 2 years).
- On concrete

(For further details on slurry handling, storage etc, see the section on 'Manure and slurry storage and pollutants').

1.26 Recycling and waste

There is no definitive list of what is or is not waste. However, agricultural waste includes discarded pesticide containers, plastics such as silage wrap, bags and sheets, packaging waste, tyres, batteries, clinical waste, old machinery and oil, etc. The new regulations are *Environmental Permitting (England and Wales) Regulations 2007*. All of the exemptions from environmental permitting are currently under review, with a formal consultation due in July 2008. A new scheme of exemptions is due to be implemented in October 2009.

As long as manure and slurry are used as fertiliser on agricultural land, then this will not be a *waste*. However, you still need to comply with the NVZ Regulations, as above. You do not need an exemption to import farmyard manure and slurry if it is to be used as a fertiliser.

Agricultural waste will have to be disposed of, or recycled in ways that protect the environment and human health. Farmers and growers will have to:

- Send or take their waste for disposal off-farm at permitted sites
- Register an exemption with the Environment Agency to recycle waste on-farm

- Apply to the Environment Agency for a permit to continue on-farm disposal

Unregulated burying and burning of agricultural waste on farms will be prohibited. The Environment Agency has produced a guidance leaflet entitled 'Stop tipping. Stop burning.' (DEFRA website, 20/5/2008).

1.27 Electrical installations - IEE Wiring Regulations (17th edition) BS 7671: 2008

There is a revised section '705 Agricultural and Horticultural Premises', some of the main points of which are included below.

- Supplementary bonding shall connect all exposed parts that can be touched by livestock. Where a metal grid is laid on the floor, this shall be included in the bonding
- Other conductive parts in or on the floor, eg concrete reinforcement, shall be connected to the bonding
- Electrical heating appliances used for breeding and rearing of livestock shall comply with BS EN 60335-2-71. For radiant heaters, the clearance shall be 0.5m.
- For fire protection services, RCDs shall be installed with a rated residual operating current not exceeding 300mA. RCDs shall connect all live conductors.
- Socket outlets must not be installed where they are likely to come into contact with combustible material.
- Socket outlets must be provided with the necessary protection.
- Where corrosive substances are present, eg in dairies, the electrical equipment must be adequately protected.
- Electrical equipment must be inaccessible to livestock. Where equipment is unavoidably accessible, eg feeding and watering equipment, this must be adequately constructed and installed.
- Appropriate diagrams shall be provided with each piece of electrical equipment.
- Wiring systems must be inaccessible to livestock.
- Overhead lines must be insulated.
- Where vehicles are operated, the following methods of installation will apply:
  o Cables shall be buried at a depth of at least 0.6m with added mechanical protection
  o In arable ground, cables should be buried at least 1m
  o Self-supporting suspension cables should be at a height of at least 6m
- Where cables will experience external factors such as livestock and mechanical shock, special conduits and trunking will be used.
- The electrical installation of each building will be isolated by a single isolation device.

- Means of isolating all live conductors, including the neutral conductor, shall be provided eg at harvest time
- Isolation devices will be clearly marked.
- Devices for isolation and emergency stopping shall be provided where they are accessible to livestock.
- Protective bonding conductors shall be protected against mechanical damage and corrosion.
- Socket outlets must comply with BS EN 60309-1
- Luminaires shall comply to BS EN 60598, and shall be selected regarding their protection against dust, solid particles and moisture.
- For high density livestock rearing, eg pigs or poultry, where electrically driven ventilation is necessary, one of the following must be provided:
  - A stand-by electrical source
  - Temperature and supply voltage monitoring. The device(s) shall provide a visual or audible signal that can readily be observed by the user, and shall operate independently from the normal supply. (BS 7671: 2008).

1.28 Other legal constraints that may be relevant

There are certain legal requirements such as under the *Code of Practice for the Control of Salmonella* concerning the keeping of crops in vermin proof stores, and the *Dairy Products (Hygiene) Regulations 1995*, affecting all milking enterprises.

The *Welfare Codes, eg Code of Recommendations for the Welfare of Livestock - Cattle,* are also highly relevant to building design, but will be discussed under the individual section headings within the text.

Section 2

CONSTRUCTION TECHNOLOGY

2.1 Concretes For Agricultural Use

Concrete is a mixture of coarse aggregate, fine aggregate, cement and water. Water is needed to hydrate the cement and provide workability of the concrete produced. Very little water is needed to hydrate the cement, if fact there is sufficient water vapour in the atmosphere to hydrate cement, given time. It is technically very acceptable to use concrete in a semi-dry state because there is more than sufficient moisture in the aggregates to hydrate the cement. Proper compaction of such a mix is the difficulty but kerbstones and the like are factory made in a heavy press machine which results in a very tough resilient product.

If laying concrete for floor slabs and aprons more water in needed in a mix to make the concrete workable, to enable accurate finished levels to be achieved and to provide a range of surface finishes. The intense difficulty is that the inclusion of too much water will leave the concrete relatively weak because any excess of water in the mix, which might be visualised as globules, will eventually dry out and leave a void within the concrete. If there are 5% such voids within the concrete the crushing strength may go down by 50%.

This is basic concrete technology and illustrates why the minimum amount of water consistent with laying methods is desirable and why compaction of the concrete to drive out any air voids is so important. There is a wide range of machinery available to compact concrete.

Within the civil engineering industry it is normal to specify the minimum crushing strength of a concrete, perhaps as a C40, which means that a concrete test piece will not fail under a load of less than $40Kn/mm^2$. This is fundamental if we are building structures like bridges and generally speaking the more cement there is in a mix the higher the resultant crushing strength is likely to be. Engineers and the concrete suppliers spend a great deal of time and effort ensuring these standards are maintained.

Within agriculture we are less concerned about ultimate crushing strength but more about durability and resistance to acid attack of the concrete. In general it may be assumed that the durability of a concrete will also rise in proportion to the amount of cement used. For this reason prescribed mixes are usually recommended. For example an RC35 mix is a recipe for a concrete mix with a specified amount of cementitious material that all suppliers will adhere to. We may also assume this mix will have a crushing strength of about $35 kn/mm^2$.

Concrete on farms is generally supplied by national ready mixed concrete companies. All the national companies subscribe to industry standard quality assured schemes which ensures the concrete delivered by truck mixer is of a consistent quality difficult to match by any 'on farm' method. These companies will readily be able to supply the various coded mixes described below.

There are other independent suppliers of concrete using mini-mixers or auger mixer trucks. They have merit in that they may sometimes be a little cheaper, or in the case of the auger mixers, mix exactly the quantity needed on site. These suppliers only tend to be economic for small quantities and repairs, and it is important to realise that in general they are not bound by the quality assured schemes as are the national companies.

Site mixing on farm is possible for small areas and volumes. Tables of various mixes both by weight and by volume are included below. Site mixing can seldom achieve the concrete quality of the national companies - mostly because of the difficulty of accurately and consistently including the correct amount of water.

Joints

As concrete sets it shrinks in volume. It is therefore important that contraction joints are included within concrete floors and roads at a maximum spacing of about 4.5 meters. It is unlikely that in the heat of the sun the concrete will ever expand back to it's original size, but it is good practice to include expansion joints at about 100 meter spacing on a farm road or similar.
It is becoming more commonplace to saw cut contraction joints with large bays within 12 hours of laying, but the risk of random cracking is increased unless protective measures are taken.

Reinforcement

The use of general steel reinforcement within concrete floors for agriculture is not ideal due to the potential danger of corrosion of the steel by slurries and effluents. In addition the effect of such reinforcement within thin slabs (less than 250mm thick) in minimal, and only has the effect of allowing larger bays to be laid between joints. The use of polypropelene fibres within the concrete mix can enhance the durability of a concrete and has a similar effect to a mesh reinforcement, also working in the third dimension. Concrete suppliers can advise.
The use of steel reinforcement may sometimes be very necessary for structural reasons such as tying in retaining walls for silage and slurry stores. It is important to maintain at least 40mm concrete cover over the reinforcement to protect it from corrosion.

Cold Weather

Care must be exercised when it is necessary to concrete in temperatures at, or below zero. Never lay concrete on a frozen sub-base. As cement hydrates it produces heat. If the work can be covered with polythene, overnight temperatures of minus 2 deg C may be endured, but no lower.

Polythene Membrane

It is always advisable to lay concrete on a polythene membrane. This prevents loss of water into the sub-base so that the cement in the mix becomes fully hydrated. It also provides a slip membrane to allow for thermal movement in the slab, minimising the effect of reflective cracking. A very thin polythene is satisfactory for this purpose although it is normal to use heavier gauges for grain stores and domestic situations.

Curing

Although concrete may visibly set within a few hours, the crystals within the structure grow and gain strength over many days. It is only assumed to be somewhere near its maximum crushing strength after 28 days. For this reason it is important that loads are not applied to fresh concrete prematurely. Also to achieve its maximum strength in situ, it is important that water is not lost from the concrete surface too quickly because it is needed to fully hydrate the cement. Depending on circumstances the concrete may need protecting by polythene or damp hessian or similar. 'Spray on' membranes are available and are very effective in difficult conditions.

Concrete Mixes

Table 2.1.1 (over page) gives an indication of the concrete mixes available for the various requirements listed. This may appear a bewildering choice but the concrete suppliers all have technical expertise and are very willing to assist. A broad interpretation of these coded mixes is as follows.

GEN 1,2 and 3 are general purpose mixes with a set minimum amount of cement used for foundations, blinding and mass concrete.

ST 2 to 5 are a range of standard mixes. They are prescriptive mixes which means all suppliers have to include a fixed, minimum amount of cement.

RC 35, 40 and 45 mixes most commonly used for floors and aprons within agriculture are also prescriptive mixes.

On a concrete delivery ticket and within this table an RC35 mix will be described as an RC28/35. The European system for crush testing concrete is to crush a small cylinder (hence 28) whereas the British Standard system is to crush a cube (35 newton). The result is the same but the notation is different.

Another difference is the European system of Consistence Class noted as S1 up to S4. This is a method of judging the workability of a concrete similar to our conventional slump test.

S1 concrete would have a target slump of	20mm
S2	70mm
S3	120mm
S4	150mm

The difficulty is that, for example, an S2 has a tolerance range of plus or minus

30mm in slump. Therefore it might be delivered as low as 40mm or as high as 100 mm and still be within specification. In all practicality the industry is likely to stay with the conventional slump concept because the parameters of the class system are too wide.

It is important that the concrete slump is specified at the time of order so that it arrives on site at the desired consistency for the task in hand. It should not be necessary to add water to a truck mixer on site. Any water added should be to 'fine tune' only. Any excess will dilute the strength of the concrete.

Selecting the appropriate concrete

Decide which of the typical applications matches your application and site conditions. Note, some soils are potentially aggressive to concrete and it is important to take this into account. If there is no professional advisor, the local Building Control Officer may be able to advise whether the local soil contains sulfates and, if so, how aggressive it is. With this information, the concrete producer may be able to advise on the correct concrete to specify.

Determine whether the concrete will be unreinforced (U) or reinforced (R) and specify this to the producer. Concrete containing any embedded metal eg holding down bolts or other steel fixings, should be specified as reinforced.

Specify the nominal maximum aggregate size only if it needs to be different from 20mm. Options, if available, will be 40 or 10mm.

The user should specify the required consistence (workability) based on the recommendations in the table.

Inform the producer of the intended method of placing and finishing the concrete.

2.1.1 Table 2: Typical applications for designated concretes conforming to BS8500-2

Typical application	Concrete designation	Recommended slump class
Concrete in non-aggressive soils (class 1 sulfate)		
Unreinforced foundations	GEN 1 (1)	S3 (2)
Reinforced foundations	RC28/35	S3
Oversite concrete	GEN 1	S3 (3)
Blinding under slabs	GEN 1	S3 (3)
Mass concrete (non-structural)	GEN 1 (1)	S3
Column bases	RC28/35	S3
Floors and roads		
Livestock floors	C28/35	S3 (3)
Stable floors	RC35/45	S3 (3)
Crop store floors	RC28/35	S3 (3)
Floors (and walls) for silage	RC35/45 (4)	S3 (3)
Sugar beet storage areas	RC32/40 (5)	S3 (3)
Workshop floors (and floors subject to small-wheeled forklift trucks)	RC32/40	S3 (3)
Brewers grain stores	RC35/45	S3 (3)
Mushroom sheds	RC32/40	S3 (3)
Toppings for floors such as parlours and dairies	RC35/45 (6)	S3 (3)
Floors (and walls) for manure and slurry stores	RC32/40 (4)	S3 (3)

Continued

Typical application	Concrete designation	Recommended slump class
External yards and roads subject to occasional de-icing salts	PAV 1	S3 (3)
Other applications		
Cavity infill to reinforced masonry	RC32/40 (7)	S3

Notes:

1. 40mm aggregate may be used in mass concrete or large foundation bases.

2. S3 slump class concrete can be used in large foundations and should be used in trench fill foundations.

3. When concreting on steep slopes, 50mm or in some cases 25mm slump concrete should be specified but this will require vibrating equipment to compact it adequately. On flat surfaces, S2 slump class may be specified if the concrete is to be compacted by beam vibrator.

4. Meets the requirements of the Control of Pollution Regulations 1991.

5. Where the concrete is subject to even occasional de-icing salts, designated concrete PAV 1 is recommended.

6. Use low consistence (workability) concretes for acid and abrasion resistance. Take care to ensure full compaction of the fresh concrete and proper curing for at least several days.

7. Use 10mm aggregate for this application.

The recommended concretes are based on 'Concrete Simplified - with designated mixes for agricultural use', and updated to reflect BS 8500.

2.1.2 Table 3: Site mixes for agricultural applications

	Alternative to GEN 1	Alternative to GEN 2	Alternative to GEN 3	Alternative to RC25/30	Alternative to RC32/40	Alternative to RC35/45
Site mixed by weight:						
Cement kg	50	50	50	50	50	50
Sand kg	160	140	115	95	90	80
20mm aggregate	240	210	195	175	160	150
Yield m³	0.21	0.18	0.17	0.15	0.14	0.13#

2.1.2 Table 4: Site mixes for agricultural applications, Continued

	Alternative to GEN 1	Alternative to GEN 2	Alternative to GEN 3	Alternative to RC25/30	Alternative to RC32/40	Alternative to RC35/45
Site Mixed by volume						
Cement	4 parts	3 parts	3 parts	3 parts	*	*
Damp sand	9 parts	6 parts	5 parts	4 parts		
20mm aggregate	15 parts	10 parts	9 parts	7 parts		

*Do not use volume batching
#Use 10mm aggregate for in-fill to cavities

For further reading refer to:

1. The New Standards for Concrete: BS EN 206-1 & BS 8500.
2. Harrison, T (2003) The New Concrete Standards - getting started.
3. BS 8500 Concrete - Complementary British Standard to BS EN 206-1

2.2 General Building data

2.2.1 Siting

Factors

- Access to roads and buildings

- Aspect, exposure and climate
- Availability of services- water, electricity, drainage, telephone and others as required
- Topography
- Management and purpose of proposals and unit
- Soil conditions

Constraints

- Mains electricity lines
- Gas, oil, water and drainage pipelines
- Watercourses
- Footpaths and bridleways
- Ancient monuments
- Scheduled buildings
- Tree preservation orders
- Sites of special scientific interest
- Areas of Outstanding Natural Beauty
- National Parks
- Nature reserves

2.3   Constructional Information

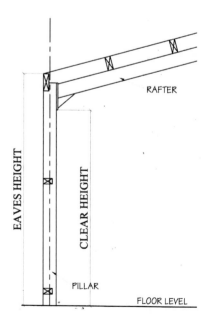

Stanchion lengths can be variable; sites should, wherever possible, be reasonably level. For steeply sloping sites excavation and/or filling may be necessary. Ground bearing pressures should be assessed and the presence of rock allowed for in the design of foundations. Allow for any future building extensions.

Adequate working space for cranes and vehicles must be provided on and adjacent to the site which must be clear of any obstructions.

Adequate water supplies and electricity must be connected. Sufficient turning space for vehicles is necessary both inside and outside buildings and the manoeuvrability of mechanical handling equipment must be assured. Storage space for materials should be available.
Always design to BS 5502- Part 2

Advantages/disadvantages - concrete/steel/timber:

- Timber may be more economical on smaller buildings and can be locally produced.
- Steel may be more economical on larger buildings but may have higher maintenance costs and does require special protection in some areas.
- Steel is the most flexible permitting a greater range of design in terms of span, bay size, length, height and roof pitch
- Fixing to timber and steel is easier and more flexible but holes need treating.

2.3.2 Foundations

- Size depends on building size, site conditions and bearing strength of the soil
- Concrete mixes see Figure 4.

2.3.3 Purlins

- Size depends on bay width
- Spacings on sheet type and wind and snow loadings
- Material used can be timber or galvanised steel.
- For some animal housing timber may be preferable due to the risk of corrosion

2.3.4 Spans

- Steel can be single, multi-spans or two level spans: 9-25m and upwards. Lean-tos (full or variable pitch available): 4.5-12.5m wide. Timber using Hardwood Portal Trusses up to 15m span. Today, spans of 40m are common, and even wider are possible. Spans have in the past been measured from outside face to outside face of the stanchions, however BS 5502 recommends that span is measured to the centre line of the stanchions for modular buildings. **Beware of this point of confusion**

2.3.5 Bay length

- 4.5, 4.8m and 6.0m are usual (but larger bays available). Bay spacing is measured from centre to centre of the stanchions and the total length of the building is taken to be the sum of the bay spacings. In fact most framed buildings will be slightly longer being the thickness of one stanchion.

Note: a lot of measurements, in practice, are still in imperial

2.3.6 Heights

- Up to 6m standard (heights can be increased in special circumstances). Eaves height is taken from the finished floor level to the plane of the upper side of the eaves beam. i.e. to the underside of the cladding material.

2.3.7 Roof Pitch

- This is variable according to air space requirements from 10°-20° (14°-16° most popular.)

2.3.8 Roofs

- Commonly the three main choices of cladding for farm buildings will be fibre cement, box profile steel or composite sheets. There are advantages and disadvantages with each.

- Fibre cement has historically been the favoured choice for farm buildings and has advantages for a number of applications. The sheets have a rough internal surface and a semi-porous nature, which makes them good for use in high humidity applications, for example livestock housing.

- Box profile steel cladding is lighter in weight and easier to fit than fibre cement, but is prone to premature corrosion if exposed to conditions of high humidity, such as those found in cattle buildings and crop stores. Heavy rain falling on steel cladding can be found to create a high level of noise inside a building and this may also be a problem in some applications.

- Composite sheets consist of two layers of steel cladding, with a layer of insulation bonded between them. These sheets are used in farm applications mainly for insulated crop stores or farm workshops. Their initial purchase cost is usually much higher than the other two options above, however they are reasonably simple to fit and compared with other methods of insulating a building, they become a more economic choice.

- The different types of cladding are available in many different profiles and colours, further information on this will be available from the cladding supplier.

KEEP THEM ALL IN GOOD SHAPE WITH FARMSCAPE

Farmscape is the fibre cement profiled sheeting that likes to keep a low profile, with its three subtle matt colours it blends unobtrusively into the rural environment. Easy to install and completely weatherproof Farmscape significantly reduces condensation to help keep grain dry and livestock comfortable. Offering excellent acoustic insulation and class O fire resistance Farmscape is also reinforced with polypropylene strips, to fully comply with the requirements of HSG 33. All this and cost effectiveness too? No wonder it's the only name in the frame.

For more information phone **01283 722588** or email **profile@marleyeternit.co.uk**
www.marleyeternit.co.uk

FARMSCAPE BETTER BY A COUNTRY MILE

MARLEY Eternit

Onwards Upwards Forwards

an Etex GROUP company

Additional factors associated with steel roofs

- All galvanised steel sheets must be stored in dry conditions on-site as they will discolour or even weld together in a solid block in time.

- Mastic sealing tape may be necessary for side and end laps where roof pitches are below 10 degrees.

- Ensure that there is sufficient ventilation in a livestock building, where non specialist sheets are used to minimise any condensation eventually attacking the underside of the sheets.

- Avoid fixing steel sheets, particularly box profile, to steel angle purlins, unless they are isolated since corrosion of the purlins will also corrode the sheet. Galvanised metal purlins are far superior in this respect.

- Salt-treated timber purlins must be isolated from metal sheeting by a layer of bitumen or DPC material.

- Always stitch sidelaps of metal and translusent sheets, particularly with the wider purlin spaces.

2.3.9 Other data

- Adaquate bracing must be provided.

- Framework and foundations will require extra strength for buildings taking thrust from bulk materials, such as grain, potatoes and silage or super-imposed loads from machinery etc.

- Steel structures are either shot blasted, primed and painted or galvanised.

- Cladding rails and purlins can either be steel, timber or concrete.

2.3.10 Table 4 Fibre Cement Sheeting Information

Sheet Type	Profile 3	Profile 6
Max. sheet length	3.05m	3.05m
Corrugation size	73.3mm	146.5mm
Cover width	651mm	1016mm
Side lap	131mm	70mm
Max purlin spacing	0.925m	1.375m
Max unsupported over-hang	250mm	350mm
Fixing point	Apex of corri	Apex of corri
Fixing type, timber purlins	Topfix for timber or drive screws	Topfix for timber or drive screws
Fixing type, steel purlins	Top fix	Top fix
Nos of fixings	2 per sheet per purlin	

2.3.11 Table 5 Details of end and side laps for fibre cement sheets

Exposure	Roof pitch	Lap treatment
Sheltered/ Moderate	22.5^0 and steeper	150mm
	15^0 to 22.5^0	300mm or 150mm sealed
	10^0 to 15^0	300mm sealed
	5^0 to 10^0. Profile 6 only	300mm double sealed
Moderate/severe	25^0 and steeper	150mm
	15^0 to 25^0	150mm sealed
	10^0 to to 15^0	300mm sealed
	5^0 to 10^0. Profile 6 only	300mm double sealed

2.3.12 Table 6: Side lap treatment for corrugated fibre cement sheets for full weather tightness.

Exposure	Roof pitch	Lap treatment
Sheltered/ moderate	15^0 and steeper	Unsealed
	5^0 up to 15^0	Sealed
Moderate/ severe	17.5^0 and steeper	Unsealed
	5^0 up to 17.5^0	Sealed

2.5 Gutter design

2.5.1 Rainfall Intensity

Rainfall intensity in the UK varies with location and surrounding topography; a rainfall intensity of 75 mm/hour is usually taken as the UK maximum when calculating the discharge requirements for gutter, downpipe and underground drainage systems.

2.5.2 Roof Drainage Requirements

The amount of rainwater collected by a given roof area largely determines the choice of gutter system to be used and the number and positioning of the outlets. It is necessary to calculate the effective area of a roof and to relate this to the draining capabilities.

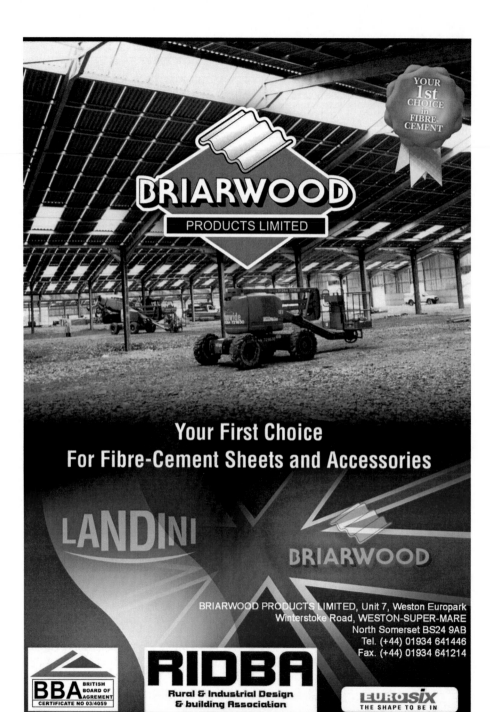

2.5.3 Gutter Flow Capacity

The draining capacity of a gutter system is determined by the gutter gradient and the size and positioning of the outlets.

2.5.4 Table 8: 112 mm roundstyle rainwater system

1:600 Fall	Outlet at centre	Outlet at end
Flow capacity	2.43 l/sec	1.3 l/sec
Max roof area	116 m²	62 m²

2.5.5 Table 9: 114 mm squarestyle rainwater system

1:600 Fall	Outlet at centre	Outlet at end
Flow capacity	30.31 l/sec	1.52 l/sec
Max roof area	144 m²	72 m²

2.5.6 Table 10: 115 mm Deepstyle rainwater system

1:600 Fall	Outlet at centre	Outlet at end
Flow capacity	4.58 l/sec	2.31 l/sec
Max roof area	220 m²	110 m²

2.5.7 Table 11: 160 mm Half roundstyle rainwater system

1:600 Fall	Outlet at centre	Outlet at end
Flow capacity	6.47 l/sec	3.23 l/sec
Max roof area	310 m²	155 m²

2.5.8 Influence of Gutter Angles

When there is a gutter angle closer than 2 m to the outlet, reduce the effective roof area that can be drained by 10%. When there is a gutter angle more than 2 m from the outlet, reduce the area that can be drained by 5%.

2.5.9 Calculation of effective roof area

2.5.10 Flat roof

For a flat roof the effective roof area is simply the plan area of the roof.

2.5.11 Sloping roof

For complex roof structures involving several or unequal slopes, a method of calculation is given in BS EN 12056-3: 2000. In the case of simple roof slopes, as illustrated below, the effective roof area is derived from the formula $E = (B + C/2) \times L$ where:

B = half roof span (m)
C = ridge to eaves height (m)
L = slope length (m)
E = effective roof area (sq m)

2.5.12 Calculation of effective roof area diagram (Figure 2)

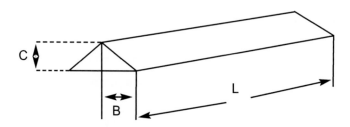

2.5.13 Effective area of Walls

Walls above abutting roofs drain on to the roofs below, adding to the amount of water which the rainwater system fitting to the roof has to convey.

2.5.14 Effective catchment area diagram (Figure 3)

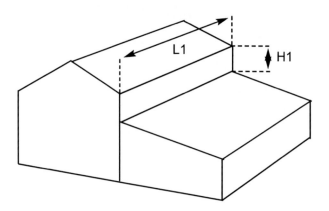

For a single wall the effective catchment area is taken to be half the area of the elevation. $E = \frac{1}{2} (L1 \times H1)$ m2

42

2.5.15 Rainwater Runoff

The amount of rainwater runoff R from a calculated effective roof area E is given by the formula:

R=0.02 I x E litres/sec

(Brett Martin, 2008)

2.6 Floors

Hardcore base

Quarried

• Granite, limestone, as raised gravels and hoggin

Others

• Slag, crushed concrete, brick, colliery shale, ashes and spent railway ballast. (Check shales and ashes for sulphate levels)

Rule of thumb

Normal depth 150mm providing a good sub-grade exists
• Geo-textile matting under
• Avoid contamination from mud below
• Compact thoroughly
• 50-100mm stone gives best sub base
• Quarried material weighs about 2 tonnes/m
• 500G polythene sheet between hardcore and concrete

2.6.1 Table 12: Classification of sub-grading for concrete and the minimum thickness of sub-base required Table - 12
BS 5502 Parts 21 and 22

Type of sub-grade (soil)	Definition	Min. thickness of sub-base required (mm)
Weak	Heavy clay, silt & peat	150
Normal	Sub-grades other than those defined by other categories	75
Very Stable	sand & gravel soils. This category includes undisturbed foundations of old roades, etc.	

2.6.2 Table 13: Suggested thickness (mm) of concrete for different sub-grades and different applications - BS 5502 Parts 21 and 22

Type of loading	Very Stable		Weak		Normal	
	un - rein	rein	un-rein	rein	un-rein	rein
Cattle, light tractors and trailers (3 tonne max axle load)	100	100	150	125	100	100
All other types of vehicle	120-150	125	175	150	150	125

2.7 Walls

BS 5502 Parts 21 and 22

The minimum widths apply only if the walls do need exceed the following heights:

- (a) 1.8m
- (b) 2.5m
- (c) 3.0m
- (d) 4.0m

The load on a foundation is produced by the height of the wall and of the foundation itself. This table does not strictly apply to buildings in which the wall supports the roof structure, although the 30 kN/m loadings can be assumed to apply to small single storey buildings with a light, small span roof.

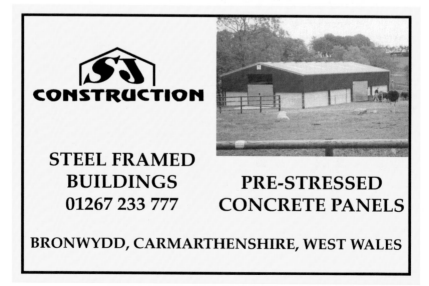

2.7.1 Table 14: Minimum foundation widths

Type of soil	Condition of soil	Field 'test' applicable	Min. width* (mm) for load indicated in kN/m		
			15	20	30
Rock	Better than sandstone, limestone or firm chalk	Requires mechanical excavator	Equal to the width of wall		
Gravel, sand	Compact	Needs pick to excavate	300 (b)	300 (c)	300 (d)
Clay, sandy clay	Stiff	Cannot be moulded in fingers; needs pick or mechanical excavator	300 (b)	300 (c)	300 (d)
Clay, sandy clay	Firm	Can just be moulded in fingers; can be dug with a spade	300 (b)	300 (c)	300 (d)
Sand, silty or clayey silty sand	Loose	Can be dug with a spade	300 (b)	450 (c)	600 (d)
Silt, clayey sand, silty sand	Soft	Easily moulded and excavated	350 (a)	450 (c)	650 (d)
Silt, clayey sand, silt sand	Very soft; avoid these sites	Exudes between fingers when squeezed	450 (a)	600 (b)	850 (c)

2.7.2 Table 15: Details of walling

Material	Uses	Type	Width (mm)	Height (m)	Construction joints (m)	Reinforcement	Remarks
Concrete blocks	Cubicles	Hollow or cellular	140	2.00	6.00	-	
	Internal walls	Solid dense	100	1.2-1.5	-	-	
	Parlour/dairy	Solid dense	140	At least 3.0	-	-	
	Loose boxes and pens	Hollow dense	215	At least 3.0	-	-	
	Strawed yards	Hollow dense	215	2.00	6.00	To 1.00m and filled	
	Slatted units	Hollow with solid wall	100	2.00 + pit	6.00	Wall beneath slats	
	Slatted slurry channels (pigs)	Hollow dense	215	2.00 or to eaves + pit	6.00	To tie into foundations	50mm of insulation + rendering
	Without slats (pigs)	Solid dense	140	2.00 or to eaves	6.00	-	
	Internal walls	Solid dense	100	1.2-1.4	-	-	50mm of insulation + rendering
	Sheep housing	Solid dense	140	2.00	6.00	-	
	Calf housing	Solid dense	140	2.00 or to eaves	6.00	-	

Details of walling - Table 15 Continued

Material	Uses	Type	Width (mm)	Height (m)	Construction joints (m)	Reinforcement	Remarks
Concrete blocks (continued)	Crop storage	Hollow 7 or 10N/mm^3	215	3.00-4.00	6.00	Cantilever retaining wall, 16mm high yield vertical bars at 225mm centres with 900mm lap bar to each course	Consult structural engineer. A 6mm mild steel
	Ventilated crop pits	Solid dense Hollow dense	100 215	Variable depth	-	- To a proper specification	Consult structural engineer
	Storage tanks	Hollow dense	215	1.8	-	To a proper specification	Bund wall must be impermeable
	Chemical stores	Cavity wall	2x100 50 mm cavity	At least 3.0	-	-	DPC needed rendered internally- 35mm cavity insulation
	Effluent settlement tanks	Hollow dense	215	Depth 2.5	-	To a proper specification	Consult structural engineer
Bricks	Cubicles and strawed yards	Semi engineering	225	2.0	Manufacturer's recommendation	-	
	Slatted units	Cavity wall tied to a semi-eng. Wall as slat support	2x100 100	2.00+ pit depth	Manufacturer's recommendation	-	

Details of walling - Table 15 Continued

Material	Uses	Type	Width (mm)	Height (m)	Construction joints (m)	Reinforcement	Remarks
Bricks (continued)	Internal walls	Semi-eng	100	1.2-1.5			
	Parlour/dairy	-	225	At least 3.0	-	-	
	Loose boxes/pens	-	225	2.00 or to eaves	-	-	
	Calf housing	-	225	2.00 or to eaves	-	-	
	Crop storage	Post tension grain wall	-	3 or 4	-	Tension beams and rods	Consult structural engineer
	Grain drier	Class B engineering	-	-	-		
	Pits and tanks	Semi-eng. With cavity	250	Various	-	Steel mesh in grouted cavity	Consult structural engineer
	Chemical stores	Cavity 50mm + insulation	250	At least 3.0	-	-	
	Silage clamps	Cavity using Class B Eng.	250	3	-	Steel mesh in grouted cavity	Consult structural engineer
In-situ	Pits and tanks	-	200	Various	-	2 layers of reinforcing mesh- 50mm under surface	Consult structural engineer
	Retaining walls	-	200	3+	-	2 layers of reinforcing mesh- 50mm under surface	

Details of walling - Table 15 Continued

Material	Uses	Type	Width (mm)	Height (m)	Construction joints (m)	Reinforcement	Remarks
Precast Concrete Panels	Pits and tanks and retaining walls		To manufacturers recommendation				
Timber	Livestock buildings	Space boarding	100 board 20 gap	From eaves to wall	-	-	
		Walls	-	2	-		
		Rail sleepers			-		
	Retaining walls	Rail sleepers	-	3+	-	-	Supported by building and stub stanchions

2.7.3 Table 16: Mortar Mixes

Mortar designation	Cement: lime: sand			Masonry cement: sand			Cement: sand and plasticiser		
	By volume	Yield (m³ per 50 kg cement)	Mean water demand (ltrs per 50 kg cement)	By volume	Yield (m³ per 50 kg cement)	Mean water demand (ltrs per 50 kg cement)	By volume	Yield (m³ per 50 kg cement)	Mean water demand (ltrs per 50 kg cement)
1	1:1/4:3	0.14	40	-	-	-	-	-	-
2	1:11/2:4-41/2	0.19	50	1:21/2-31/2	0.15	35	1:3-4	0.16	40
3	1:1:5-6	0.25	70	1:4-5	0.21	45	1:5-6	0.24	50
4	1:2:8-9	0.37	100	1:51/2-61/2	0.27	55	1:7-8	0.30	60

2.7.4 Table 17: Quantities of units and mortar needed per 100 m² of wall

Unit work size (mm)	No. of units	Wall thickness (mm)					
		90	100	102.5	140	190	215
440x215	988	0.59	0.66	-	0.92	1.25	1.42
390x190	1250	0.67	0.74	-	1.04	1.41	-
215x65	5926	-	-	1.76	-	-	4.52
290x90	3333	1.17	-	-	-	3.34	-
190x90	5000	1.31	-	-	-	3.62	-
190x65	6667	1.59	-	-	-	4.18	-

2.8 Water supply

Please refer to BS 5502 Part 25

All water supply installations should comply with the Model Water Byelaws 1986.

For all major new developments the design of the water distribution system should be entrusted to a competent mechanical services engineer.

When a new supply is required from the Water Authority's main, it is desirable to obtain as large a diameter supply as possible to reduce the drop in pressure as the water is distributed around the unit.

- Fittings must be serviceable and not produce waste, undue contamination or excessive consumption
- Fittings of dissimilar metals must not be used to avoid corrosion by electrolytic action
- Private and public supplies must not be connected together. Use a cistern to seporate both.
- Pipes and fittings inside and outside buildings must be placed and protected to minimise frost and mechanical damage.
- Underground pipes must be at depths between 750mm and 1350mm to reduce the risk of freezing.
- All exposed water pipes should be protected from frost with insulation and/or low voltage heating cables. Where necessary the insulation or heating cables must be protected from damage by livestock and other mechanical damage.
- Drinking troughs must be fitted with a ball valve or other flow control devices. Supply pipes must be 25mm above the top edge of the trough or valve.
- Water Authorities often require water storage equal to the anticipated daily consumption to be installed. This may be one large tank serving the whole farm or smaller tanks in the individual buildings where the water is to be used. Storage tanks should be insulated.
- Storage cisterns should be positioned so as they can easily be cleaned and inspected. A non-airtight cover should be provided to keep out light, dust, vermin and birds. Inlet pipes must be at least one pipe diameter higher than the overflow.
- Seven days notice is required by water authorities for inspection before back filling trenches.
- No pipes should pass into, or through, any ash pit, manure pit, sewer, drain, cesspool or refuse chute or any manhole used for these purposes.

- Pipes should not be laid in or on any foul soil that is likely to cause undue deterioration of the pipe, unless it is effectively protected from contact with that soil or material.

- No pipe should be used if it is of material susceptible to permeation by any gas which could cause contamination of the water in the pipe. Pipes should not be stored in a position where such permeation could occur.

- Water bowls, drinking troughs etc. must be supplied from storage tanks, not direct from the main.

- Stop-cocks should be installed to allow each section of the installation to be isolated so that repairs can be undertaken with the minimum of disruption.

- Polyethylene pipe should be black for above ground use and blue for below ground to distinguish it from gas pipes and electricity cables. Pipes can also be made of copper and unplasticised polyvinylchloride.

- Joints:

Copper-	Solder or compression
Polythylene-	Plastic or copper
CR-	Dezincification fittings for underground use

2.8.1 Table 18: Water requirements for types of stock

Animal	Range
Cattle	10 - 150 litres/day
Sheet	5 - 20 litres/day
Pigs	5 - 25 litres/day

2.9 Boreholes

Creating a borehole begins with a survey of the area to be drilled and the likelihood of discovering an aquifer, within the required parameters, and which will yield a sufficient amount of water. The results of the survey will enable an informative decision to be made as to what depths drilling will be needed; this is a determining factor in the overall cost involved.
Once that has been done, a 150mm diameter hole is drilled to the required depth; this is lined with a well screen, which makes up part of the filter system. Once this is established (one to two days), a high-pressure pump is installed to bring the water to the tap, which can be installed almost anywhere. (For best results, keep the tap within 5m).

The cost of a borehole can vary depending on the depth, type of strata being drilled and materials such as pump, well screen and filter pack. For this reason, a full-survey is necessary prior to any pricing of a system is made. As a guide, a full working borehole with pump and control unit can be made for £2500.

2.10 Drainage

BS 5502 Part 25

All drainage work should comply with BS8301 as far as it is applicable.

Two, three or even four separate drainage systems are often needed on a farm:-

1.   A 'clean' water system which conveys roof water and any other unpolluted water for discharge into a watercourse stream etc- or (very occasionally) to a soakaway system.

2.   A 'domestic foul' system which collects the 'domestic' sewage from the dwellings and toilets in the offices etc and conveys it to a public sewer or, more commonly in the case of farms, to a septic tank. This system is subject to Building Regulation Control and must be approved by the Local Authority's Building Inspector.

3.   A 'slurry' system which collects slurry and heavily polluted water and conveys it to a reception pit and storage tank prior to subsequent treatment and/or disposal. In NVZ areas 5 months storage is becoming a requirement.

4.   A 'dirty water' system which collects lightly polluted water-parlour washings etc- and conveys it to settlement tanks prior to disposal by low-rate irrigation.

Where more than one drainage system is required, great care is needed in determining the levels of the drains. Generally one system is laid below the other ensuring that there is adequate difference in levels at the points where the pipes cross- generally the difference between invert levels at a crossing point should be at least 50 mm greater than the diameter of the lower pipe. Which system is the lower depends on the topographical features, the levels of ditches, the depths of slurry reception pits, etc. If the 'dirty' water system is to take drainage from a parlour pit it has to be accordingly deep.

Plastic pipes are commonly used for all types of system. They are bedded in pea-gravel'. If the tops of the pipes are less than 600mm deep the pea-gravel may, if loadings dictate, be covered with concrete (GEN 1) 100mm thick. Diameters of pipe depends on the volumes to be carried. Pipes carrying unseparated slurry should not normally be less than 225mm diameter.

Manholes or rodding points must be installed at every marked change in direction or gradiant and possibly at every junction.

2.11 Electricity

Always use a competent electrician and take advice from the local electricity company.

Electrical definitions:

Volts (V)	The electrical pressure at which electricity is delivered- the voltage. This causes the current to flow. Normally 240V single phase or 415V three phase.
Ampere (A)	The rate of flow of a current through cable or item of equipment caused by a given pressure in volts.
Watts (W)	Electrical power or load. The rate at which an item of electrical equipment will take power from the supply. W=VxA. 1 hp= 0.75 Kw
Ohms (Ω)	The resistance of a conductor. V $\div$ A=Ω
Kilowatt (kW)	1000 watts
Kilowatt hour (kWh)	A unit of electrical energy (one unit of electricity)

Do's and don'ts for Electricity

Do's

- Employ an electrical contractor approved by the National Inspection Council for Electrical Installation Contractors when carrying out any wiring installation.

- Ensure that electrical installations comply with the IEE Regulations (Regulation for the Electrical Installations)

- Ensure that everyone involved in the use of electricity is fully informed of the safety requirements.

- Use only electrical equipment and accessories designed to cope with the prevailing conditions that conform to BS 4343 and IP 54 or higher specification.

- Cover unprotected fixed equipment and switches with waterproof sheeting when hosing or steaming.

- Carry out regular inspections and maintenance.

- Test RCD's (residual current devices) regularly and visually examine the associated earth wire, especially after a lighting storm.

- Arrange for immediate replacement or repair of damaged wiring or accessories.

- Ensure that extension leads are uncoiled from their drums before they are used.

- Use properly constructed (purpose made) extension leads if extra cable length is needed.

- Ensure when making electrical connections that terminal screws are fully tightened.
- Make sure that cable grips in plugs are securely tightened.
- Switch off and lock off and/or unplug equipment before starting maintenance or repairs. Such work should only be undertaken by electrician.
- Keep motors, ventilated fans and airways free from dust and debris.
- Check thermostat settings frequently.
- Use electrical equipment and accessories designed to cope with prevailing conditions.
- Clean electric tools and their flexible cables before use and store them in a clean dry place.
- Learn the dangers from overhead lines and underground cables.
- Take care when moving long objects near overhead lines.
- Follow equipment manufacturer's instructions.
- Contact an electrical contractor when in any doubt about the safety of electrical equipment or the installation.

Don'ts

- Extend or modify existing wiring installation, this is a job for a competent electrical contractor.
- Pile bags of fertiliser or other obstructions close to main switches and so make it difficult to switch off quickly in an emergency.
- Use wrong size or 'make do 'fuses.
- Extend cable or flexible cords by means of temporary joints.
- Overload circuits or flexible cords e.g. by using multiple adaptors.
- Route trailing leads where they are likely to be damaged.
- Allow long flexible leads to become a permanent part of the installation.
- Wire plugs to flexible leads which have non-standard colours, seek advice.
- Connect infra-red heating lamps to lighting circuits.
- Use portable type radiant heaters (domestic type) in damp conditions such as in a milking parlour.
- Adjust the setting of circuit overload devices or make adjustments within control panels.
- Use resistance regulators for controlling the speed of fans for the control of lighting.
- Connect portable electric tools to lighting circuits.
- Connect a portable generator to an electrical installation (except in

properly designed connection points)- this is a job for an electrical contractor.

- Erect stacks, clamps or buildings under or close to overhead lines.
- Move tall machinery under or in the vicinity of overhead lines until the clearances have been checked safe.
- Assume that the overhead line conductors which have fallen are dead.
- Use faulty equipment or circuits. If in any doubt, switch off and call in an electrician; remember electrical shocks can be fatal.
- Use bayonet type adapters.
- Attempt to carry out electrical repairs, employ a competent electrician.

2.11.2 Electricity Supply Information

Electricity is distributed around the country using high voltage lines and cables and is then reduced in voltage through transformers. Many farms are served by their own transformer which is usually mounted on a high overhead line pole.

The supply to farms is either single phase (240 volts) or three phase (415 volts). Farms which only use electricity for domestic use, lighting and small motors may have a single phase display. This is characterised by two or three overhead lines (conductors) from the transformer to the farm. Farms which use more electricity, especially for large motors (e.g. for grain handling) or for heating are likely to have a three phase supply. This is characterised by four or five conductors entering the farm. Single phase equipment can be connected to a three phase supply. Single-to-three phase converters allow three phase motors to run on a single phase supply provided the single phase supply is adequate. The need for this might occur, for example, on farms when new machine is required which has three phase motors built in. Where new motors are being purchased it is usually preferable to select them to suit the supply available.

The transformer size is the main factor here limiting how much electricity can be taken by the farm and, therefore; must be considered when new electrical equipment is to be installed.

If extra electrical equipment is required it may be necessary to increase the supply. This is called 'supply reinforcement'. It may involve upgrading the existing single phase or three phase supply or changing from single phase to three phase. This involves work by the Electricity Company in uprating lines, cables, transformers, meters etc and is often chargeable to the customer. Changing from a single phase to a three phase supply will also necessitate alterations to the electrical wiring on the farm itself.

When changes are planned, the first step is to determine what extra equipment is to be installed and include a reasonable allowance for future expansion. Then consult the Agricultural Engineer of the local Electricity Company (his services are free) who will determine whether or not supply reinforcement is necessary. If it is he will prepare a quotation. Obtaining a quotation and wayleaves, obtaining planning and other consents, and getting the work done can take time- so start early.

All electrical installations should be in accordance with the latest edition of the IEE Wiring Regulations and carried out by contractors approved by the National Inspection Council for Electrical Contracting.

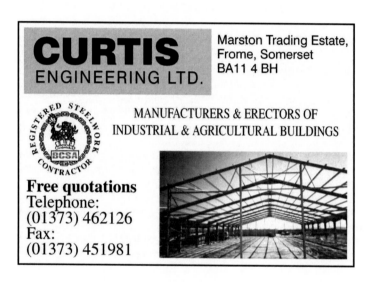
2.12 Lighting   Refer to BS 5502 Part 20

Example from Figure 4 over page

7.5   9.0
[←2→] ←2→ indicates that, between 7.5 and 9.0m from eaves for a totally enclosed bay, with 3m eaves height, the area of roof light required is 2.0 m².

7.5   9.0
[6→] 6 → indicates that the total area of roof light needed for a roof 9.0m from eaves to ridge, for the same building, is 6.0m².

2.12.1 Roof light areas per bay (Figure 4)

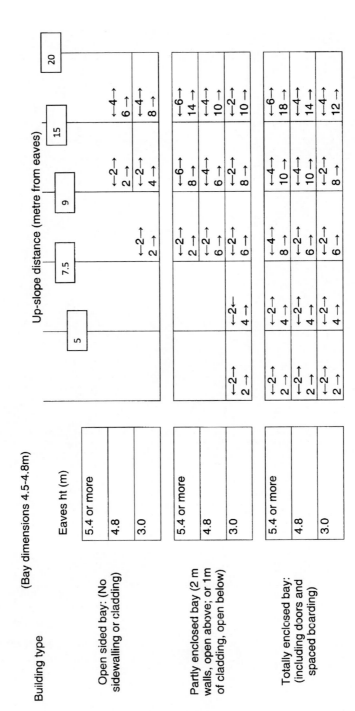

(Bay dimensions 4.5-4.8m)

Up-slope distance (metre from eaves): 5, 7.5, 9, 15, 20

Building type	Eaves ht (m)
Open sided bay: (No sidewalling or cladding)	5.4 or more
	4.8
	3.0
Partly enclosed bay (2 m walls, open above; or 1m of cladding, open below)	5.4 or more
	4.8
	3.0
Totally enclosed bay: (including doors and spaced boarding)	5.4 or more
	4.8
	3.0

59

OUR ROOFLIGHTS CAN BRING MUCH MORE THAN JUST NATURAL LIGHT INTO AGRICULTURAL BUILDINGS

Natural light in agricultural buildings encourages healthier, more disease resistant livestock and provides a better working environment for farm workers, resulting in improved productivity all round. Installing 20% of the roof area in rooflights provides sustainable light energy, reducing energy costs and CO_2 emissions. So they are kinder to your pocket and the environment too.

They need to be the right rooflights, of course, and at Brett Martin we have the biggest, most advanced and sustainable range under the sun. Our agricultural range includes Trilite GRP and Marlon CS polycarbonate corrugated sheet to meet any profile; many guaranteed for 25 years, ensuring your rooflights continue to perform for years to come.

Contact us today for information and advice on achieving the optimal daylight conditions for your agricultural facility.

Call: 024 7660 2022 **Email:** daylight@brettmartin.com

2.12.2 Table 19: Artificial Lighting Levels

	Standard service illuminance - Lux	Notes
Task and Inspection		
Inspection of farm produce where good colour rendering is needed.	500	Careful choice of fluorescent tube light
Other inspection tasks where additional lighting is needed; lighting of visually difficult tasks	300	Using local lighting Where milk is handled or stored
Milking premises	500	
General Lighting		
Farm workshop	100	Plus task lighting Where frequent veterinary attention is given.
Sick animal pen	50	Veal units as for other buildings
Baby calf nursery	50	
Other farm and horticultural buildings		
Where adequate daylight is provided.	20	A 5% daylight factor is adequate Except as note (d) below
All others	50	

The above, Table 19, must be read with the following notes:

A,   In animal buildings and other places (apart from this specified in the table) a low illuminance level may be employed for animal welfare purposes. Horticultural buildings may, however, require higher illuminance for productivity purposes. But when operators are present, lighting must be provided to at least the standards of the table.

B,   The standard service illuminance is that used for design purposes. A service illuminance is an average over the area throughout the life of the installation. The standard service illuminance is the recommended service illuminance for the application and may apply to the whole area or only to the task area. When measuring, values will be found that exceed the mean, with others below the mean. The illuminance at a point is measured by holding a lightmeter in the plane of the work at working plane height.

C,   In any building where extra illuminance is needed temporarily to aid the performance of a task, extra localised lighting should be brought into use. This lighting equipment should be capable of producing an illuminance of at least 300 lux on the task and its immediate background. It is recommended that the task lighting should be additional to the general lighting indicated in the table.

D,   In farm buildings not provided with a 5% Daylight Factor, a standard service illuminance of 50 lux is required, but where a windowless building is entered through a vestibule which excludes daylight, provided the vestibule has a standard service illuminance of 50 lux, acting as a light/dark adaptation zone, the main building may be lit to a standard service illuminance of 20 lux, as required. In the case of pig and poultry houses, however, care should be taken to ensure that the standard of general lighting does not encourage aggressive vices in the stock.

2.13 Energy Supplies

The main source of energy on the farm is electricity being easily installed, reliable within the level of power provided, flexible in use and operationally clean. However, it is not always the cheapest and it can become expensive if a new supply has to be provided or an existing one upgraded. Other sources of energy could be available.

Before starting work on any improvements or alterations to any buildings make sure that whatever the source of supply provided to the farm that it is sufficient to cope with any resulting requirements.

2.13.1 Gas

Mains gas supplies are not normally available in country areas but consult British Gas on availability. If a supply is available it must be brought onto the property to the meter point by British Gas. Any subsequent appliances and supply pipes should be inspected by them. Take their advice and only use a British Gas trained and approved installation contractor. Make sure that all supplies are well protected, do not interfere with any supply and report any leaks immediately to British Gas.

2.13.2 Propane Gas (LPG)

An alternative to mains gas is propane gas. Again only have it installed by approved fitters and protect the supply pipes. Storage of the gas must be in a properly designated container which is rented from the gas supplier. The container may be above-ground, or below-ground. Under-ground tanks are particularly good in areas where a hidden tank has advantages. Once buried, the area can be returned to grass or planted with flowers.

The container must be placed on a level concrete pad which is sited in the open and which has a good access for delivery vehicles. An ordering system is available from certain suppliers which ensure that bulk tanks can be automatically topped up without the landowner having to remember.

This has much lower installation costs compared with oil, and many companies can take all responsibilities for installation, maintenance and safety of the tank.

LPG is a versatile fuel that can be used for central heating, catering and heating water.

LPG burns cleaner than oil, producing fewer carbon emissions, less smell and less smoke.

2.13.3 Heating Oil

Heating oil should be stored in a properly approved and designed tank and be raised on piers to ensure that the oil flows by gravity. The tank should be bunded in the same way as it is required for agricultural fuel oil (see Control of Pollution (Silage, Slurry and Agricultural Fuel Oil) Regulations 1991). The tank should be placed in the open with a good access for delivery vehicles and with a concrete pad for this vehicle to stand on whilst filling the tank. The concrete pad should slope to a drain connected to an oil interceptor trap.

2.13.4 Table 20: CO_2 and carbon emissions for common heating fuels in buildings

Emissions	Kg CO_2/kWh	Kg carbon/kWh
LPG	0.19	0.052
Oil	0.26	0.071
Solid fuel	0.30	0.082
Electricity	0.44	0.12

2.13.5 Telephone

Mobile phones can be used, but their effectiveness will depend largely on proximity to a transmitter. They may also prove more expensive than installing a permanent land-line. All lines to the farm will be provided by the telephone company. If possible put all of them underground, in particular across accesses. Do not put telephone lines and electricity supplies in the same duct if they are installed underground.
Installation of telephones can be by DIY but this will depend on the system

installed. Any systems using a form of exchange should be installed by the supplier.

2.13.6 Broadband

Broadband internet is anything from 10 to 150 times faster than traditional dial-up internet connections, and is available to more than 99% of UK homes.

Broadband doesn't tie up your phone line and you pay by the amount you download or upload rather than any time you spend online, so you can leave your internet connection on permanently if you want to.

2.13.6.1 Types of Broadband

- **ADSL**

  o Most homes can access broadband through BT's copper-wire phone network. This type of broadband is known as Asymmetric Digital Subscriber Line or ADSL broadband. ADSL broadband is available to more than 99% of UK households, although the broadband speed you'll be able to get will vary depending on where you live.

- **Cable**

  o Cable broadband, only available from Virgin Media, provides an equivalent service to ADSL broadband, using cable phone lines instead of BT's network. Cable broadband is available to about half of UK homes, mostly in urban areas.

- **Mobile**

  o O2, Orange, Three, T-mobile, Vodafone and Virgin Media now offer services whereby you can access broadband on your computer via the 3G mobile signal. The technology is very new and depends on there being a 3G signal, but may offer hope to anyone who can't get broadband via ADSL or Cable.

- **Networking your broadband**

  o To share your broadband with more than one computer, you can use a rooter (with built in modem). Routers rend to be more expen sive than standard modems though the price difference is narrowing rapidly.

- **Wireless**

  o In order to do away with countless wires, wireless modems and routers are becoming increasingly popular and cost from around £50. They fulfil the same function of normal modems or routers but without the need for wires trailing all over the place.

Section 3

BUILDINGS FOR LIVESTOCK PRODUCTION

3.1 Slurry, Manure, Dirty Water and Silage Effluent

3.1.1 Environmental Protection and Waste Management Regulation

With ever increasing interest in environmental protection and as agriculture is increasingly brought into line with other industries so far as waste management and pollution controls are concerned, then so the design and construction of facilities and systems for managing livestock waste must be undertaken with greater care and attention to detail.

In 2006/7 a wider tranche of waste management regulations was applied to agriculture and has formed the basis for the need for Waste Management Licensing exemptions and permits for a range of waste types. However, so long as livestock manure or slurry is properly utilised in accordance with good agricultural practices and without risk to the environment, this material need not be categorised as agricultural waste, whereas e.g. plastics, scrap metals, construction materials and vegetation residues are covered by the statutory controls and are subject to a regime for storage, handling and a 'Duty of Care'.

The Regulations, Permits and Exemption regime is policed by The Environment Agency and extensive information is provided through their office network and their web-site: www.environment-agency.gov.uk

Note: Pollution Regulations and support agencies vary in Scotland, Wales and Northern Ireland.

3.1.2 Statutory Controls for Livestock Waste Management

Even though the livestock waste may be managed separately to other wastes, the risks for slurry and manure causing point source and diffuse pollution are very high. Consequently there are three key aspects that are vital to any new structural design or scheme of management. Besides from these, there are planning and Health and Safety considerations.

3.1.3 Health and safety considerations for livestock waste management

1. Structural Integrity to minimise the risk of failure of slurry/effluent/dirty water containment.
Refer to: 'The Control of Pollution (Silage, Slurry and Agricultural Fuel Oil) Regulations 1991 (and as amended 1997)' and British Standards (BS) 5502: e.g. part 50: 1993 (Livestock Slurry Tanks)

2. Storage Capacity, to avoid need to apply slurry etc. during times when diffuse pollution is a major risk.
Refer to: Nitrate Pollution Prevention Regulations (England) 2008 (established in response to The EU Nitrates Directive)

3. Management systems to avoid direct or indirect pollution of watercourses.
Refer to: The Water Resources Act 1991 and Water Act 2003 and subsequent Regulations for the protection of Surface and Ground Water.

3.1.4 Basic Information Required to Inform Decisions in the Design Process

To establish the viable options for managing livestock manure, there are many parameters, ranging from the livestock type and accommodation to the weather and geographical location. It is useful to assemble the necessary information prior to listing all of the options; in this way some options can quickly be eliminated and the cost-benefits of the preferred options can be more accurately calculated.   The following provides a summary of the key considerations.

a) Livestock Type, number, growth stage (size) of animals and feeding regime
b) Accommodation type, period of housing and the bedding material and quantity used
c) Drinking water, wash water and other water ingress to the system (e.g. ground water)
d) Climate and Weather, especially rainfall where unroofed yards contribute to the quantities needing to be stored and managed.
e) Land availability (cropping, soil types, slope, drainage and topography)
f) Existing systems and infrastructure, where the new facilities are to be integrated.
g) Future expansion/reduction of herd/flock size or other diversification plans

3.1.5 Assessing slurry and manure quantities

Points a) and b) provide the key information on which the volumes of slurry or manure are calculated. A useful reference is provided within the help sheets that accompany the NVZ regulations. Tables of data are available showing a) the excreta types and volumes for each animal type at a range of growth stages or productivity levels. When this data is combined with b) the period of housing and adjusted depending on the bedding type and quantities used the aggregated seasonal output of slurry or manure can be determined. Spillage of drinking water or wash water or rainfall dilutes the slurry or leads to drainage from manure, therefore an assessment of c) and e) are important. The information will show how to calculate the volumes of excessive rainwater entering the system, based on exposed yard areas multiplied by rainfall factors.

3.1.6 Assessing dirty water quantities

In systems where dirty water from pen washing, dairy/parlour washing and exposed yard areas can be kept separate from slurry and manure, the volumes can be regarded outside of the NVZ calculations, but, owing to the risks of pollution, the standards of management still need to be maintained in keeping with the Control of Pollution (SSAFO) Regulations.

3.1.7 Example calculation for Slurry and/or Dirty Water storage requirements

- Figure 26 provides a table showing the Volume (m3) of slurry output per livestock type (or place) per month. When you have multiplied the numbers of each animal, by the number of months when they are housed (housing period), then adjust this for situations where not all of the animal output is collected as slurry (some may be collected within a bedded FYM system). I.e. set the figure to 1 for all collected as slurry, 0.5 for half collected as slurry.

- Estimate the average monthly rainfall onto the farm during the 5 months (cattle farms) or 6 months (pig/poultry farms) storage periods.

- Calculate the amount of rain falling directly onto the uncovered or unroofed existing slurry store, and onto concrete areas draining into the slurry store. Include all fouled concrete areas and dungsteads if the run-off drains into the slurry store. Exclude run-off from clean yard areas and roof areas if rain falling on these is collected and discharged to a clean drain. Measure yard areas in metres, and calculate the overall square metres of area (estimate and then multiply length X width for each part to give square metres, and then add all the parts of the yards together). Use the Met Office websites, or local weather data to find average monthly rainfall (wintertime), this will be in mm, multiply by the months required, then by the yard area (sq. m.) and divide by 1000 (to correct for the mm) and the result will be cubic metres (cu.m i.e. m3).

- The sum of the slurry, the wash water, rainwater to the yards and rainwater direct to the store provides the total volume of slurry (including dilution) that needs to be stored. Don't forget to adjust your calculations if:

- You always export some of your slurry to another farm during the storage period.

- You always use a mechanical separator to remove solids from the slurry. Reduce the volume of cattle slurry by 15 - 20%, and reduce the volume of pig slurry by 5 - 10%.

- Note: Remember to build in an allowance for the freeboard (0.3m free

68

board for rigid tanks; or 0.75m for earth banked systems)

• Typical wash water use from high volume hoses is 0.9m3 per month (30 litres per cow per day); or from low volume hoses is 0.6m3 per month (20 litres per cow per day).

• Wash water on pig farms is estimated as: Sows incl. litters 10.0; Maiden gilts and boars 0.6; Weaners 2 - 2.6; Growers & Finishers 1.9 - 1.6 litres per pig place per week in each case.

• Livestock slurry, or effluent containing even low concentrations of slurry cause oxygen depletion in water (due to biological oxygen demand - BOD) which is why it is an offence to permit manure, slurry or effluent to enter surface waters; and is why in part that there are new rules regarding aquifer protection. Silage effluent contains very high concentrations of sugars and other materials (very high BOD) that make it extremely polluting if allowed to enter water courses. Nitrogen rich effluent is also toxic to fish due to the ammonia concentration.

3.1.8 Establishing an outline scheme for waste management

The availability of land for spreading or applying livestock manure or slurry is essential for sustainable livestock keeping and is why the new rules regarding the balance of stocking numbers with productive land areas and cropping type have been introduced. As grass and arable crops have a range of nutrient requirements and vary in their tolerance to slurry or manure applications then the overall system must be planned so that the application rates, logistics and timing are balanced with crop requirements and pollution prevention. Farmyard manure (FYM) may be applied in the autumn (subject to application rates to service the crop requirements and avoiding smothering on grassland), but poultry manure and other slurry types may not be allowed due to the risks of nitrogen losses to groundwater (NVZ rules).

Thus the overall scheme should be drawn up so that a complete and integrated solution comprising reception, transfer, storage, treatment logistics and land application is possible. As the scheme is developed, the benefits of the various options can be evaluated and the constructional details and dimensions of each component can be specified within the design.

3.1.9 Table 21: Slurry produced per month (based on undiluted slurry)

Livestock type on slurry or part-slurry based system	Volume per animal place per month, m^3	Livestock type on slurry or part-slurry based system	Volume per animal place per month, m^3
Dairy Cattle		**Cattle**	
1 dairy cow, large (600-700kg)	1.95	1 suckler cow, large (550-600kg)	1.37
1 dairy cow, small (400-500kg)	1.61	1 suckler cow, small (400-500kg)	0.97
Heifer, up to 12 months (310kg)	0.61	1 grower over 24 months (to 600kg)	0.97
Heifer, 13 to 24 months (580kg)	1.22	1 grower, 18 months (to 550kg)	0.79
1 bull beef animal, 3 to 15 months (490kg)	0.79	1 grower, 12 months (to 440kg)	0.61
1 calf, 2 months (to 65kg)	0.21	1 bull for breeding, to 24 months (550kg)	0.79
Pigs		**Pigs**	
1 sow place, including litters	0.33	1 weaner pig place (13 to 30kg)	0.06
1 maiden gilt place	0.19	1 grower pig place (31 to 65kg)	0.11
1 boar place	0.35	1 finisher pig place (66 to 100kg)	0.16
1 weaner pig place (7 to 12kg)	0.04	1 finisher pig place (30 to 100kg), wet meal fed	0.22
Sheep		**Sheep**	
1 adult ewe with lamb	0.13^d	1 store lamb	0.03^d
Poultry		**Poultry**	
1 000 laying hens	3.50	1 000 broiler breeder pullets	1.22
1 000 free range laying hens	2.80	1 000 broiler breeders	3.50
1 000 broiler places	1.82	1 000 male turkey places	4.87
1 000 layer pullet places	1.22	1 000 female turkey places	3.65
Solid manure (FYM) production	For FYM either use your knowledge of the amounts of straw/bedding used, or use the simple multiplication factors, which use the excreta (slurry) output values as the basis.		
Dairy Cow FYM	multiply the total excreta volume (m^3) by 1.3 to get the FYM in *tonnes*		
Beef cattle, Pigs and sheep FYM	multiply the total excreta volume m^3 by 1.15 to get *tonnes*		

3.1.10 Consideration of a wide range of Manure and Slurry Management Options

When starting afresh, it is very useful to consider as wide a range of options as possible. The list at table 22, over page, provides a basic summary of options.

The table is not comprehensive and new developments are made as new situations arise. Also, it is necessary to consider new options where an initial treatment process results in by-products or a different quality/ consistency of manure or slurry.

Notes for: Table 22: Livestock Manure and Slurry Scheme Components (over page)

a   Temporary storage on fields is permitted under NVZ Regulations, provided the location is varied each year and other pollution risks (effluent) are mitigated.

b   Typically the bedded area will be provided with nominal amounts of straw, sand or sawdust which over time enters the slurry in the passageway.

c   The performance of slurry separators vary, however, the wet solids removed from mixed slurry may account for 20 % of the volume and is managed separately.

d/e   The liquid separated from weeping wall and strainer box type compounds is regarded as slurry, and needs to comply with NVZ rules as slurry.

e   Strainer box or walled systems, enable combined storage of the solids and liquid fractions; and enable the liquid to be extracted/ sucked out as appropriate.

f   Kennel type systems provide some segregation of the bedded area (strawy manure) from the wet but lightly strawed slurry in the passageways.

g   The NVZ rules allow for the drainage of liquid from scraped strawy manure to be regarded as slurry and the solids, when stackable to be regarded as FYM.

h   In some deep pit systems, where there is excess drinker leakage (or bird health reasons) then the manure will be quite wet and form a thick slurry.

i   The effect of the ventilation air of modern layer housing, provides early drying of the manure on the belts, before it is offloaded to the manure storage area at the end.

j   Broiler litter has a high nitrogen content and so must comply with NVZ 'closed periods' of (non-autumn spreading), however temporary field heaps are acceptable.

k   Silage effluent is high in nitrogen, but also strongly acidic. Dilute with water before application but beware that if mixed with slurry, then H_2S will be evolved.

l   The pollution regulations class dirty water, containing excreta or urine as 'slurry'. Being low in nitrogen, it may be regarded separately under NVZ Regulations.

3.1.11 Table 22: Livestock Manure and Slurry Scheme Components

Origination of Manure or Slurry	FYM	Slurry	Semi-solid	Poultry litter	Stirring & mixing	Slurry Separation	Dilution	Drying	Aeration	Composting	Digestion	No-treatment	External Maure pad	Roofed manure bunker	In-situ Storage	Temporary field heap	Steel tank	Concrete Tank	Concrete Panel Compound	Weeping wall compound	Strainer box/ walled Compound	Earth banked lagoon	Earth banked Compound	Specialist effluent tank	Rear-Discharge FYM Spreader	Dual Purpose manure spreader	Rotary side spreader	Tanker	Pump & Umbilical	Pipeline & sprinkler/jet	Splashplate outlet	Boom & splashplates	Boom and dribble outlets	Distributer and drop hoses	Dribble outlets	Trailing shoes	Injectors	Autumn applied	Spring/summer applied	Utilised on farm	Exported off farm	As fuel for renewable energy	Domestic/landscaping use
Dairy cows on deep straw bedded yards	x									x		x	x	x	x	x									x	x	x											x	x	x	x		x
Dairy cows in cubicles		b			x	c	x		x		x	x					x	x	x	d	e	x	x		x	x	x	x	x		x	x	x	x	x	x	x		x	x	x		
Suckler cows on deep straw bedded yards	x									x		x	x	x	x	x									x	x	x											x	x	x	x		x
Suckler cows on slats		x			x	x	x		x		x	x					x	x	x	x	x	x	x		x	x	x	x	x		x	x			x	x	x		x	x	x		
Pigs on straw bedded yards	x									x		x	x	x	x	x									x	x	x											x	x	x	x		x
Pigs on slats		f			x	x	x		x		x	x					x	x	x	x	x	x	x		x	x	x	x	x		x	x			x	x	x		x	x	x		
Pigs straw bedded with scraped slurry	f				x	x	x			x		x	x	x	x	x	g		g	g	g	g	g		x	x	x	g											x	x	x		
Laying Hen (poultry)- deep pit	x	h	x							x	x	x	x	x	x	x									x	x	x											x	x	x	x		x
Laying hen (poultry)- belt system	x		x					i		x	x	x	x	x	x	x									x	x	x											x	x	x	x		x
Laying hen (poultry)- barn/free range	x									x	x	x	x	x	x	x									x	x	x											x	x	x	x		x
Broiler chickens on litter				j						x	x	x	x	x	x	x									x	x	x											x	x	x	x	x	x
Sileage Effluent					k												x	x						x							x	x											
Dirty water		l			x	x	x		x			x					x	x				x						x	x	x	x	x			x			b	x	x	x		

3.1.12 Features and benefits of various system components

System component and features Materials handling and transfer	Other considerations and benefits
Hydraulic, or chain or cable based automatic scrapers. Semi-solid slurry in cubicles, yards and passageways.	Efficient, low power consumption and low labour input. Regular checks and servicing of the scrapers is vital to avoid breakdowns.
Tractor scraper semi-solid slurry in cubicles, yards and passageways.	Tractor scraper semi-solid slurry in cubicles, yards and passageways.
Tractor + loader/ telescopic loader solids and semi solids.	Very versatile, can operate in many different situations, for clearing passageways or yards. Very effective for loading spreaders or keeping middens stacked high and tidy.
Slatted floors with below ground tanks or slurry channels. Slat configurations and dimensions vary depending on animal types and care must be taken in selection to avoid animal feet problems. Slats can work well in pig systems where the dunging areas are over the slats and separate from the bedding areas. Ventilation is important to ensure that there is no adverse gas build up. In cattle housing, it is essential to avoid silage effluent entering the below slat slurry store as the gases given off can cause severe health problems.	Slats provide a simple and non labour intensive means of removing the slurry from the living areas as it is deposited. Also with the storage of the slurry being under the housing, then rainfall into the store is avoided. Good systems will incorporate simple means for removal of the slurry at reasonable intervals, and may comprise an end sluice for gravity emptying to a store, or else provide fixed suction points for vacuum tanker removal of the slurry.
Free flow slurry channels Normally laid about 1m wide by 1m deep, laid level and can be any length, but they should be stepped down by 150mm every 25m. At each step and at the discharge end of the channel there must be a 150mm high raised lip so as to retain moisture and to keep the slurry flowing.	Simple means for providing intermediate storage and initial mixing prior to pumping slurry to a storage tank. When reception pits are sited so that they can be accessed by a tractor and a slurry tanker then they provide more options for means of emptying and for 'desludging'. Check site for rock and ground water problems.

Ramps The slope on any ramp should not exceed 7° or 1-in-8. The width should not be less than 2m between 225mm square kerbs and they must be safety fenced with an end-stop comprising a 150mm x 75mm mild steel channel fitted across the end.	Used in conjunction with a tractor mounted scraper, ramps provide a simple means of filling a part or fully sunken storage compound. The length can be reduced if use can be made of sloping ground.

System component Slurry and manure treatment systems	Other considerations and benefits
Mechanical mixers, either screw propeller types mounted on long booms that reach over the top of a tank or compound, or similar types fitted on a support, against the side wall of a tank.	Tractor mounted types are versatile due to their mobility and can easily be extricated from work if they became clogged. Also they can be relocated within the same tank, compound or lagoon so that all of the stagnant areas (corners) are dealt with.
Bubbler mixers. Types include large bubble mixers that impart a localised physical mixing action above each nozzle; and fine bubble aerators that generate a fizz of fine bubbles over a wider area, which creates a pattern of recirculation within the tank as well as better oxygen exchange between the air and slurry liquid therefore mitigating mal-odour formation.	Low operating cost and easy to switch on or off as required, and therefore the stored material can be maintained in a stirred state during the season. Bubblers also impart an element of conditioning and aeration that may mitigate odour formation. Poorly managed or aggressive aeration of a stagnant slurry can cause mal-odour release.
Recirculation pump mixer. Contemporary jetters either re-circulating above or below the slurry surface. They draw slurry from the tank, through a chopper pump and jet the liquid back onto the surface or back into the mid-height region of the tank, to provide stirring effect.	Rather a course means of achieving the stirring and mixing of the tank contents, pumped jetter systems can be used to break up a crust, but the process is time consuming and energy intensive.
Weeping walls. These are normally built above ground level on a concrete base that is extended beyond the walls, with a channel to collect the liquid which is then taken to a tank. Use of upright RSJ supports combined with	Weeping wall stores provide the combined functions of de-watering and storage. However, as the new rules deem the liquid to be slurry (not dirty water) and modern techniques tend towards storage of the extracted

horizontal sleepers, with 25mm wooden spacers is common, but the modern systems are normally constructed of precast concrete panels typically 2 to 3m high with vertical slots 25 to 35mm wide.

liquid rather than low rate irrigation, the emphasis has changed and designs have evolved so that storage of the liquid is given greater emphasis. Vertical slotted walls have been found preferable to the older horizontal sleeper types as they are self clearing and maintain a steadier flow.

Strainer boxes and strainer walls within a compound. As an evolutionary development of simple earth banked or concrete walled compounds, such systems combine the merits of weeping walls, within a single system. When slurry is contained within a store for a few months, it stratifies into layers with silt on the bottom, then liquid and then the fibrous floating material at the top, as a thick crust. A strainer box at one corner, or anywhere within the store, provides an extraction point for the liquid when the time is appropriate, e.g. late spring time. When the liquid is removed, the fibrous solids and silt will continue to dry out with the benefit of the capillary action, wind and warmer temperatures and an element of in-situ composting. The solids form a 'soft cheesey' consistency which can be spread as a farm-yard manure when conditions and timing allows.

The 300mm freeboard must be allowed for, but if this is at risk, the contents can be lowered by removing liquid from within the strainer box.

Modern systems use large rectangular compounds that include a false weeping wall across one end. The gap of 2m or so between the false wall and end wall, provides a large volume of containment of the liquid fraction. Typically, with the benefit of a concrete ramped entry at the upper (opposite) end, then the solid manure residues can be easily loaded to spreaders within the store. Design the ramp the ramp with a rough finish to provide traction. Otherwise the solids may need to removed by excavator, in which case the dimensions and accessibility at the side walls should be specified so that the contents can be safely reached by the machine.

Mechanical separators.
There are a number of different types of separator on the market and the choice will depend on the consistency of the material to be handled and the required quality of the separated solids (e.g. stackability and moisture content) and percentage solids remaining in the liquid. The separator must be sited adjacent to the reception pit, have an adequate electricity supply, tractor access to remove the solids and

The solids separated from slurry may comprise up to 20 % of the volume and so the storage requirement of the liquid can be reduced accordingly. The separated liquid provides several benefits:

Less likely to cause siltation or crusting in store:

•   Easier to pump, aerate or

Mechanical seperators - cont. either a temporary or permanent storage tank for the liquids. Frost protection and structural strength of the support stand are two key factors in the design, but ultimately the key consideration is reliability in adverse conditions. As the stacked separated solids may generate further effluent caused by rainfall, the overall scheme should include measures to prevent this is an inclusive part of the design. E.g. making provision for the solids to fall direct to a trailer or manure spreader for early removal to the fields may be a useful option.	stir, • More uniform in quality and nutrient content, • Much less likely to cause scrorch or solids contamination when applied to silage crops, • Reduced odour, • And better infiltration into the soil giving better plant nutrient utilisation.
Aerators These systems work best on the liquid fraction after the slurry has been separated. Solids in the waste increase the amount of oxygen needed and also increase the amount of energy required for mixing. The most efficient method is to use small bubbles, by blowing compressed air through the porous diffusers with very small outlets. There are wide range intensities of treatment ranging from simple maintenance of aerobic conditions to offset mal-odour formation, to prolonged and maintained treatment i.e. 'liquid composting' where the results are long lasting; or the short but much more intensive treatments aimed at solving short term odour problems, e.g. odours during land application.	To be successful, the systems require: A constant and well mixed volume of slurry each day. A slurry DM content of less than 3 %. Bedding material should be kept out. Suitable oxygen concentration throughout the treatment tank. Sustained steady state treatment of slurry by aerobic biological treatment is capable of reducing odour emissions during and after land application by up to 90%. Such systems are expensive to operate and therefore where aeration is undertaken, it tends to be low intensity to provide mixing and maintain aerobic conditions.
Anaerobic digesters (AD) AD is a process which harnesses natural anaerobic bacteria to treat biodegradable materials and produce 'biogas,' which is approximately 60% methane and which can be used to generate heat and if required can run engines to drive electricity generators.	The digestate residue from this process is usually a pumpable material that can be further separated into a fibre and a liquid. Digestates can be beneficially applied to land as a fertiliser and/or soil conditioners. When used in conjunction with a

AD breaks down solids biologically and therefore serves to reduce solids content within the slurry. Systems are capital intensive and require the expert assistance to define the feasibility, the payback and the overall economic viability in relation to the type, quantity and value of the energy and bi-products produced.

The processing of slurry in an AD facility must be fully authorised, and depending on the range of materials being digested, an Environmental Permit may be required.

mechanical separator, an AD process enhances the benefits of the separator, and provides a measure of odour control and bio-security.

$1m^3$ of cattle manure typically produces up to $20m^3$ of biogas, and the calorific value of this gas will be $5.83kWh/m^3$. Allowing for engine and generator inefficiencies, the following would be required, for 1 kW of continuous electricity to be generated by a biogas fuelled engine and generator set:

10 cows	to generate	1 kWe
100 pigs	to generate	1kWe
1,000 poultry	to generate	1kWe

Composting facilities

Composting is the breakdown of organic wastes by micro-organisms, in the presence of air, to produce water, carbon dioxide heat, and a more stabilised, pasteurised organic material.

A facility usually comprises a large concrete pad, where the material is laid out in large windrows (2-3m high, 3-5m wide and 25-40m length), side but side with a small gap between, to allow effluent drainage.

The process comprises the preparation of a fresh windrow at one end of the pad, and each week or fortnight the removal of the oldest windrow and the far end of the pad. Each windrow is consecutively turned 'down the pad', creating a space for its successor to be turned into. Four or five windrow spaces where each windrow resides for a fortnight provides 8 to 12 weeks of composting, in which time the material will become sanitised and conditioned to form a friable soil like

Useful 'gate-fees' or revenues can be earned from providing commercial composting services, but there are significant costs and statutory controls.

Most farm composts are made from green waste, such as hedge trimmings and tree prunings, or livestock manures and slurry. The compost can be sold for use as a soil conditioner to improve soil structure and enhance its biological activity.

The use of compost reduces harmful emissions of greenhouse gas (methane) from landfills, and returns organic matter to the soil.

The benefits of composting are:

- Provides a measure of bio-security.
- Improved quality consistency of the solids.
- Reduced pollution risk in store and during application.

Composting facilities - cont. material, high in nutrients and with minimal odour. In many instances traditional composting of FYM is undertaken simply by moving or turning the manure heap in-situ. This has the same effect as the large scale commercial operation, but with lesser input costs but a lower level on control.	• Friable material spreads better with reduced risk of smothering or leaf contamination. • Minimises toxicity effects in the soil. • Is marketable and may provide useful revenue from the public.
System component **Slurry and manure storage systems**	**Other considerations and benefits**
Above ground circular steel stores These tanks are used for separated liquids **and** whole slurries. The concrete base for these and the erection of the tank must be carried out strictly in accordance with the manufacturer's specifications. On many sites it is advisable to have a structural engineer's report on the ground bearing strength of the soil, and the depth and type of hardcore required.	An electricity supply to the tank will be required in most cases. Regular inspection of the tank, particularly the inside, is required to ensure that deterioration is not occurring. Filling of the tank is normally over the top. Emptying is through the side via two lockable in-series valves (present for safety and security). In calculating the size of tank, remember to allow for the 300mm freeboard requirement. Consider a system such as aeration or mixing to reduce odours and to stop a crust forming.
Circular concrete stores These tanks are used for separated liquids and whole slurries. Attention to the foundations and structural design is similar to the steel tanks.	The benefits of concrete stores are the robustness, ability to partly construct them below ground level and their resistance to corrosion.
Rectangluar concrete stores These may be designed with up-slope entry points or ramp loading systems and may incorporate weeping walls. They can be used for whole slurries, semi-solids separated liquids or even part or whole FYM, provided there is a means for	The designs may very if very liquid material is to be stored as the means of sealing joints is more sophisticated, however, the simpler free standing concrete panel type stores are robust, versatile, can be partly below ground level, provide

emptying. Attention to the foundations and structural design is similar to other steel or concrete tanks.

resistance to corrosion and enable hybrid systems with weeping walls or strainer boxes to be incorporated into the design, together with secondary compartments for segregating the solids and liquids during the storage term.

Earth banked compounds

The site suitability is paramount, as those on sandy soils or where there is a high water-table are unsuitable. Structural design must be a qualified engineer so that the banks are impermeable. Structural stability has to be achieved which requires proper construction. A freeboard of 750mm must be allowed for.

The store may be constructed as a drive-in store with angled base or ramp leading down to the deepest part, or a fully-sealed enclosed earth bank, where emptying is done over the top of the bank by suction or by excavator.

Often this may seem like the easiest and cheapest option for slurry storage, but there are various points that should be considered if they are to meet the requirements of the Regulations.

The store must be large enough to store all dung, urine, bedding, dirty water and other liquid to be stored, and rainfall for the total storage period.

The base should slope slightly to the filling point. Access should be provided around the banks so that the compound can be emptied and a safety fence must be erected around the outside.

Dirty water containment

This normally operates from a three-chambered below-ground tank with H-pipes between the chambers and the liquid being pumped onto the land by means of a static or mobile irrigator. As with other tanks, the walls and base can be cast in-situ or can be precast concrete, but must be impermeable.

A number of earth banked lagoons can be used on suitable sites but the rain landing on the lagoon will add to the capacity and pumping requirements. An emergency overflow should be provided leading to additional storage. An allowance for freeboard is required. Tractor access for desludging should be considered and an electrical supply to operate the pump will provide efficiency during land application.

Silage effluent

This is normally stored in below-ground tanks, either concrete or GRP (according to SSAFO Regs). GRP tanks must be carefully and properly installed and anchored down to avoid

Pre-cast concrete tanks are now available that will meet the regulations. The size requirement given in the SSAFO Regs is for two days supply and even for wilted

them lifting out of position.	silage this volume is less than the total effluent produced.
System Component **Slurry and Manure Spreaders**	**Other considerations and benefits**
Rear discharge FYM spreader.	Modern makes have high capacity, very strong hydraulically variable speed chain and slat moving floors and optional tail-gates prior to the heavy duty augers.
Dual purpose side discharge spreader.	Taken over from the rotaries to some extent, these provide for slurry and semi-solid manure spreading, easier filling, higher capacities and more uniform application with fewer wheelings.
Vacuum tanker and optional discharge equipment.	Provide self loading from pits, sumps as well as tanks and compounds. Wide range of capacities, hydraulic gates and controls and large floatation wheel options.
Slurry pump and pipeline, (umbilical cord) and optional discharge equipment	Slurry pump and pipeline, (umbilical cord) and optional discharge equipment Commonplace, as they minimise wheelings, improve workrate and reduce compaction damage. Various options for the application equipment, see below.
Discharge equipment options	
Single spreader splash-plate.	Simple, new designs provide downwards trajectory to minimise emissions, and improve spread pattern.
Boom and multiple spreader splash-plate.	Improve working with compared to single device, improves spread uniformity and can be compatible with tramline widths in cereal crop spring time applications.

Tool bar and multiple dribble/trailing hoses.	Trailing hoses are simple but need monitoring for blockages else the application can be uneven. With consistent separated liquids these provide a cost effective solution, minimise emissions, and are simple to operate.
Shallow injectors.	Conventional injectors designed to work at rootzone depth, to minimise soil disturbance, but bury the slurry to mitigate odour nuisance. Faster and with less soil heave than deep injectors and with less stress and weight on equipment.
Trailing show injector.	Modern innovations that provide slurry placement under the leaf canopy, (minimising ammonia release and avoiding scorch) with sufficient disturbance of soil to assist penetration, without soil heave or damage to roots.
Low rate irrigation The regulations allow for short term storage and frequent land application of dirty water (not effluent or slurry) provided the land type and soil are suitable and a management plan is implemented. Such systems may make use of sprinklers, low trajectory jets, or winched along travelling irrigators (rotating booms, static booms or jet systems). Alternately, there is the option for dirty water to be stored with the slurry which means that the mixed liquid is dilute enough to reduce crust formation and the material can be pumped and distributed more easily, e.g. through hose or pipeline systems. Use of underground field irrigation systems is not advised, due to the potential for settlement and sedimentation blockages within the pipes.	Little and often low rate irrigation systems may reduce the overall capital expenditure by reducing storage requirements. A simple three section settlement tank with adequate buffer capacity can provide a relatively low cost system so that a low powered positive displacement plump (progressive cavity type) can be used with hose pip-lines (50-63) and boom or jet type irrigators. The alternative is to utilise the services of a contractor, to empty out dirty water lagoons and tanks, using a large capacity pump, pipelines and umbilical pipeline system feeding a tractor mounted boom and splashplate spreading system. Dirty water can be used beneficially when grassland is short of water, or on a silage aftermath, when the next dressing of fertiliser may be 'washed in' to the soil in order to provide faster grass re-growth.

3.2 Designing for Natural Ventilation

Providing adequate ventilation in a building for livestock is probably the single most important factor to be considered at the design stage of a new building if the stock housed in the building are to thrive and achieve their optimum performance potential.

There is much historical data to assist today's building designers, however, there are many factors (often outside the designer's control) that will affect the ventilation of a building. Factors which should be considered include:

- the location and local topography;
- the proximity of other buildings and their relationship to the building in question;
- the size and number of stock to be housed within the building at any one time; and,
- the physical dimensions of the building in question.

In addition to the above, the needs of the stockman i.e. so that s/he can complete his/her task(s) in comfort and without risk to his/her health, should also be a considered, as should the potential for damage to the building structure and fabric should the internal environment prove to be undesirable.

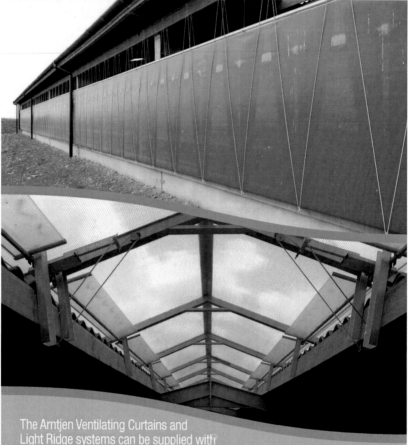

3.2.1 Design Principles

There are two natural forces which operate to provide ventilation in buildings; these are the "wind effect" and the "stack effect".

At wind speeds greater than about 1 - 2m/s, the stack effect is largely overcome and the ventilation is dominated by wind. In practice this means that buildings are ventilated by wind for most of the time. However, most ventilation problems that do occur in naturally ventilated livestock buildings occur during calm, still conditions i.e. when there is no wind blowing. Therefore, natural ventilation system design procedures virtually ignore any wind effect and concentrate on the minimum ventilation rate that occurs under the stack effect alone.

The principles governing stack effect are fairly simple, but the calculation required to apply it to livestock buildings is relatively complex. Stack effect operates on the principle of thermal buoyancy, which is the difference in weight between two columns of air caused by their difference in temperature. Therefore, in a building, warm air rises and is replaced by colder, denser air from outside. The critical factors governing ventilation due to stack effect are the height of the air column i.e. the difference in height between inlet (normally below eaves height) and outlet (normally the ridge height), and the power to drive the system i.e. the heat generated by the stock (i.e. metabolic rate). In addition, the outside temperature and thermal conductance of the fabric of the building will also influence the overall stack effect.

A detailed design method, produced by the Scottish Farm Buildings Design Unit (SFBIU), in approx 1980, is reproduced below, with up-dated graphs, taking into account the increased live weight of stock. You can use this to calculate the required openings for a specific building.

3.2.2 SFBIU Ventilation Openings Calculator

This method of calculation provides the **minimum** areas required for adequate, natural ventilation during still conditions. It applies to a ventilation system with openings at the eaves and an open ridge, with at least difference in height of 1m between them.

In order to assist in describing this method of calculation, the following example is used:

The building is 26m wide and 46.8m long with a 15° roof pitch. It has a central feed passage. 120 cows are housed in two groups of 66 cubicles on either side of the feed passage, i.e. there are 10% more cubicles than cows. The cows' average weight is 600kg.

3.2.3 To calculate the width of open ridge required.

Step 1. Calculate the total floor area per animal (A), including all passageways.

$$= \frac{\text{Total building area}}{\text{Number of cattle}} = \frac{26 \times 46.8}{120} = 10.14 \text{ m}^2/\text{animal}$$

Step 2. From Graph (1) below, using live weight and total floor area per animal, find the outlet area (A'out). A is 10.14 m²/animal and live weight is 600kg.

Therefore, A'out = 0.15 **m²/animal**

However, this is the outlet area for a building with a height difference of 1.0m between inlet and outlet. This needs to be corrected for the actual height difference of the building.

Step 3. Calculate the actual height difference, H.
From the table below, it can be seen that a 15° roof pitch has a rise of 1 in 3.7.

$$\text{Height difference, H} = \frac{0.5 \text{ span}}{3.7} = \frac{13}{3.7} = 3.5$$

Step 4. From Graph (2) below, find the height correction factor, h.
For a height difference of 3.5m, h = **0.55**

Step 5. Multiply A'out by the h factor to give the corrected open ridge area per animal. A'out x h factor = actual open ridge area per animal

0.15 x 0.55 = **0.0825 m²/animal**

Step 6. Calculate the total area of open ridge required.
Area of open ridge per animal x Number of animals

0.0825 x 120 = 9.9m²

3.2.4 Table 23: Relationship between roof pitch and size

Roof pitch in degrees	10	15	22.5	30	45
Rise	1 in 5.5	1 in 3.7	1 in 2.44	1 in 1.72	1 in 1

Step 7. Calculate the width of open ridge:

$$= \frac{\text{Total area of open ridge}}{\text{Building length}} = \frac{9.98}{46.8} = 0.212\text{m} = 212\text{mm}$$

In practice this would be specified as a nominal opening of 225mm

SEE RIGHT and OVER LEAF FOR GRAPHS AND MEASUREMENTS

GRAPH 1

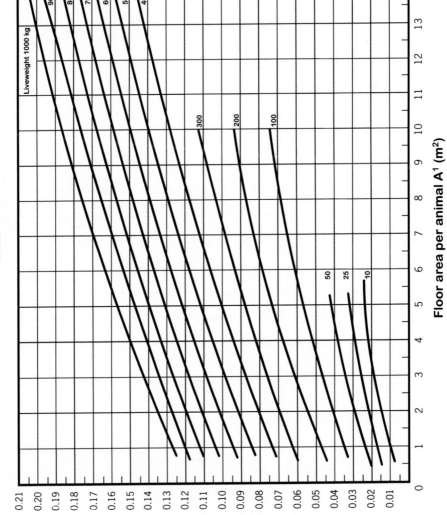

GRAPH 2 Height Factor

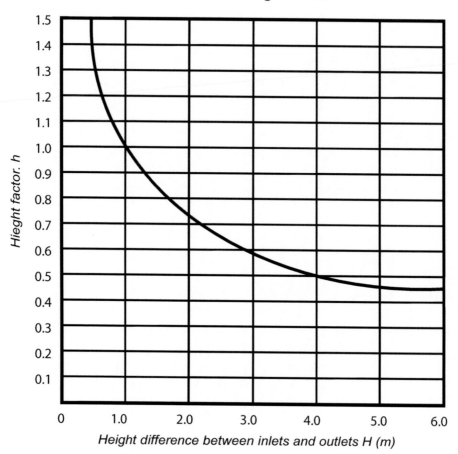

Height difference between inlets and outlets H (m)

y-axis: Hieght factor. h

3.2.5 Calculate the inlet area

Step 8. Inlet area = outlet area x 2, which could be provided by a continuous gap equal to the required open ridge, below each eaves i.e. on both sides of the building. However, this solution is not likely to be satisfactory as it may cause draughts at stock level. Therefore, to find an equivalent spaced boarding area, assuming 20% void area i.e. 100mm boards with a 25mm gap, the depth of spaced boarding required at each eaves is:

$$\frac{\text{Inlet area}}{\text{\% void area}} = \frac{0.225}{0.20} = \textbf{1.125m}$$

Therefore, the required, unobstructed, depth of spaced boarding is 1.125m

The usual arrangement of openings in a portal frame building is ideally an open ridge, or protected open ridge and using some form of wind break material (typically spaced boarding or a plastic mesh or even just a gap) below the eaves.

In mono-pitch buildings of less than 10m span (depth) an open front will usually provide sufficient inlet and outlet space. However, where the span is above 10m additional openings at the rear may be necessary.

It is vitally important to design inlets and outlets such that they do not cause draughts at stock level. However, special arrangements to avoid this i.e. lids at the back of pens, positioned below the inlets, yet above the stock, which effectively create a sheltered and protected lying area for the stock, may help prevent a draught problem.

On large span portal frame buildings, particularly where the eaves height may not be sufficiently high to provide the necessary depth of draught free inlet, it may be necessary to adjust the height of the building at the design stage, or consider an alternative form of inlet. Furthermore, an alternative solution could be to consider forming a 'breathing roof', i.e. by forming slots in the roof slope which will provide both an inlet and outlet function and supplement existing ridge and eaves openings. This solution is particularly useful for improving the ventilation in existing buildings and providing ventilation in multi-span buildings where the central areas are usually very difficult to ventilate when using normal eaves inlets and ridge outlets.

3.3 Buildings for Dairy Cows

3.3.1 General

It is very important that dairy cow housing provides a comfortable, clean, dry lying area that is well drained and gives each cow adequate space and ensures that welfare standards are fully met, be these as required in the Welfare Codes or a Quality Assurance Scheme. In general, the accommodation should enable all the animals to move around freely i.e. between the lying, the loafing, the feeding and the milking areas, in whatever order is required, without risk of injury and bullying from other stock.

Dairy cows are typically housed in cubicles (sometime called 'stalls' in mainland Europe and USA) or other loose housing systems, such as straw yards. The most common construction material is steel framed buildings with steel cubicle divisions and concrete floors, walls and passageways. However, buildings, such as kennels (i.e. a cubicle house where the divisions are extended to support the roof structure) and smaller span buildings are often constructed using timber. Lactating cows should not be accommodated in wood chip corral systems, or similar, as they are intrinsically dirty environments.

The animals are usually housed in groups for ease of management. Group size will be dependent on the number of cows in the herd, the milking system, the expected yield and state of lactation of each cow, access to feed and the need, or not, to access grazing in the summer, as well as management preferences. Research has shown that cows are likely to be less stressed if they are housed in groups of less than 60 cows, but it is possible, where the herd is large and good welfare and management systems are employed, to have groups well in excess of 100 cows. As far as possible, groups should be matched taking into consideration the above factors and building constraints. It is common to replace between 10% and 25% of the herd each year, as cows get old and yield drops etc. this may also influence group sizes.

The tables below can be used as a guide to the minimum space that should be provided for each cow in a loose housing system, such as a bedded yard (i.e. straw).

3.3.2 Table 24: Recommended minimum area allowances for dairy cattle housed in bedded yards. BS5502 Part 40

Liveweight (kg)	Bedded area (m²)	Loafing area (m²)	Total area per cow (m²)
200	3.5	2.5	6.0
300	4.5	2.5	7.0
400	5.5	2.5	8.0
500	6.0	2.5	8.5
600	6.5	2.5	9.0
700	7.0	3.0	10.0
800	8.0	3.0	11.0

N.B. For wholly bedded yards the total figure should be used.

3.3.3 Cow Cubicles

A cubicle is formed between two divisions which define the lying space for each cow. The lying space for each cow is further defined by use of a brisket board positioned on the base of the cubicle at between 1.6m and 1.8m from the kerbstone (heelstone). The brisket board's function is to prevent a cow from lying too far forward in the cubicle. Proprietary products are typically made from rubberised plastic, but timber rails or tubular steel bars have been used with some success. The correct position a cow, before she lies down in the cubicle, is achieved by using a head rail which is fixed near the front of the cubicle, roughly directly above the brisket board and at a height of between 1.1m and 1.3m above the base (i.e. approx. 200mm below withers height).

Cubicle divisions are typically made from tubular, galvanised steel, but can be formed from timber or other appropriate material (i.e. concrete). Where cubicles have to cater for cows of differing age and size, the cubicle dimensions should be chosen to accommodate the average of the largest 20% of the herd and if possible cubicle divisions that provide good space sharing should be used i.e. cantilever divisions that do not have supports at the rear which could restrict cow movement and cause injury (see illustration below).

Designers should allow between 5% and 10% more cubicles than the number of cows in a group, or house. Check the QA scheme for particular requirements.
Cows require space in front of them to enable them to lie down and, in particular, to get up again (lunging space). Where this is not provided, cows may not use the cubicles or will try to gain space from the adjacent cubicle, if the division will allow this. Alternatively, where there is sufficient space between the divisions the cows will attempt to lie diagonally between the divisions. It is advisable to provide adequate space (i.e. length and clear distance between divisions) as indicated in the table below.

Cubicles should be raised above the adjacent passageways to prevent waves of slurry flooding the lying areas when the passageways are being scraped. In general this should not be too high as to cause the cow difficulty entering, but typically a kerbstone height of 150mm is adequate. The cubicle base should fall from the front to the back (2% - 3%), as this will allow some drainage of liquids and some movement of bedding, where this is used.

The base of a cubicle is typically made from concrete. However, the surface of the base should be: comfortable for the cows to lie on; prevent and not cause injury; easy to clean and maintain; and, cost effective. Such comfort can be achieved in any number of ways, but typically this is by using a reasonable amount of bedding i.e. straw or commercially available mats or mattresses. However, the latter can be very expensive and may still require a minimal amount of bedding (sawdust or similar) to soak up small amounts of moisture that may be carried onto the bed on the cows feet. Where thick mattresses are used in a cubicle, this should be taken into account when considering the kerb heigh

3.3.4 Table 25: Guidelines on cubicle (stall) dimensions

Liveweight (kg)	Min base length (open front) (m)	Min base length (closed front) (m)	Clear width between divisions (m)
200	1.75	1.90	0.75 - 0.85
300	1.85	2.10	0.85 - 0.90
400	1.95	2.20	0.09 - 1.00
500	2.05	2.30	1.00 - 1.10
600	2.15	2.40	1.10 - 1.20
700	2.25	2.55	1.20 - 1.30
800	2.35	2.65	1.30 - 1.40

Call for your Free
Roundhouse DVD

Every building we erect, has one thing in common...

The
Roundhouse
Roundhouse Building Solutions Ltd

...a great team of people!

Whatever your Farm building needs are, our team are on hand
to help you, from planning to construction

Call us now, on 01833 696 927
or visit www.s-and-a.co.uk

The **Simpson & Allinson** Group of Companies

N.B. Cubicles are considered 'open front' when they are in a row facing another row of cubicles (i.e. so called head-to-head) or they face a passageway and hence, assuming appropriate positioning of rails etc. and no high walls are constructed at the cubicle front; occupants can gain lunging space directly in front of them. Closed front cubicles have restricted head room or lunging space i.e. the cows face a wall or solid barrier.

3.3.5 Feeding and Drinking

In a straw yard, the distance from the bedded area to the feeding area (within the same building or elsewhere) should be as short and as direct as possible, thus avoiding slurry being spread over a wide area. However, where a straw yard adjoins a feed stance, the straw yard area should be rectangular and preferably much longer than it is wide, with the maximum distance from the back wall to the feed stance being no more than 10m and cow access to the feed stance is along as much of its length as possible, this will then avoid excessive poaching of the bedded area. Form a kerb of at least 150mm along the edge of the bedded area, particularly at the entrance/exit to the straw yard and feed stance, this will help retain bedding and avoid contamination of the lying area with slurry when scraping the feed stance.

In general, a feed stance should be at least 3.6m wide, i.e. sufficient distance to allow cows to walk behind cows that are feeding without disturbing them. Where cows have to enter and exit cubicles onto a feed passage, the passage should be increased to be at least 4.8m wide, thus allowing cows' easy access to the cubicles at the same time as the feed barrier.

Water troughs are an essential feature in any dairy unit. Cows in peak lactation, particularly during the summer months, may require in excess of 150 litres of water each day. It is recommended that there should be sufficient water trough space for at least 10% of the herd to drink at any one time. Trough space can be considered to be the same as for feeding (see table below).

Water troughs are usually positioned in cross passages and the return route from the milking parlour. However, their position in bedded yards/areas requires careful consideration, to avoid excessive spoilage of the bedded area; in this case it is best to position them along the side of the feed stance that joins the bedded area. Here they should be surrounded by a wall, or solid screen, on three sides (i.e. in the bedded area); such that cows can only access the water trough from the feed stance. Tipping water troughs allow easy maintenance of the trough and a fresh supply of clean water for the cows to drink. They may also assist cleaning of the floor around the trough when they are emptied onto the floor, thereby making the slurry more liquid.

There are numerous types of feed barrier available, ranging from inclined dovetail to a simple horizontal bar. The barrier is a means of separating stock from the tractor passage and should allow reasonable control of stock as they feed. Where necessary, a feed barrier containing locking yolks can be used to aid the day-to-day management of cows i.e. if a cow requires treatment, she can be enticed to the barrier with some extra feed and then secured and either treated at the barrier or released and taking to a handling/holding area for later treatment. The tractor passage should be around 5.0m wide, including a trough of at least 500mm width on both sides of the tractor passage. To assist cows to eat the feed, the feed troughs should, ideally, be raised above the feed stance by at least 100mm, and no more than 300mm.

3.3.6 Table 26: Feed trough lengths required for dairy cows feeding simultaneously -ADAS 2006

Liveweight (kg)	Feed trough length (mm/hd)
200	400
300	500
400	550
500	600
600	670
700	700
>800	750

NB: Where cows have unrestricted access to feed the trough length per head may be reduced significantly (i.e. by up to 75%). However, this may cause aggressive behaviour and mean that timid cows do not get the required amount of feed.

Cows may be fed a complete diet at a feed trough, or given additional rations using an automatic system such as an 'out-of-parlour-feeder' (OOPF). Check manufacturers' recommendations, but in general allow for up to 40 cows per each automatic feeder. Automatic feeders vary in their space requirements but, in general they are a similar length to a cubicle and slightly narrower (i.e. 2.8m long by 800mm max.). They will also require a storage bin, for the concentrates, to be positioned nearby and with good lorry access for filling. Some form of auger system is then used to convey the concentrates from the storage bin to the OOPF.

3.3.7 Passageways

Most QA schemes and BS5502 part 40, require a minimum of 3.0m² loafing area per cow to be provided in any building, to promote appropriate welfare and encourage hoof wear and good cow foot condition. This can be provided as a separate area or allowed for in all the passageways that the cows' access, this may mean that the minimum passage widths quoted here may have to be increased to achieve the required loafing area.

Passageways between cubicles should be at least 2.5m between kerbstones. Where large cows are housed in cubicles, the passage width should be at least equal to the base length of the cubicles, thus allowing cows' sufficient room to access and exit the cubicle and not disrupt other cows using the passageway. As an absolute minimum, the passage width should be sufficient for two cows to pass, side-by-side.

Cross passages are used to allow cows' access to other areas of the building or unit, e.g. a feed stance or a collecting yard for milking. They should be level and provide a sure footing for the cows i.e. not too rough, but not slippery. Short, link, cross passageways i.e. between a cubicle passage and feed stance, should be raised by 150mm above the cubicle passage level, so that waves of slurry do not enter them unnecessarily. Alternatively, if slatted passageways are used, this problem can be avoided, but this may have to be offset against welfare issues with using slats.

In general, cross passages should be a minimum of 2.4m wide. However, they are often used as a convenient place for positioning water troughs, in which case, they should be at least 3.6m wide, which will allow cows to pass behind cows that are drinking. There should never be 'dead-ends' formed in lines of cubicles. Therefore, there should always be a cross passage at both ends of a cubicle house. In long buildings, cross passages should be formed roughly every 20 cubicles along the length of the building.

CUBICLE TYPES

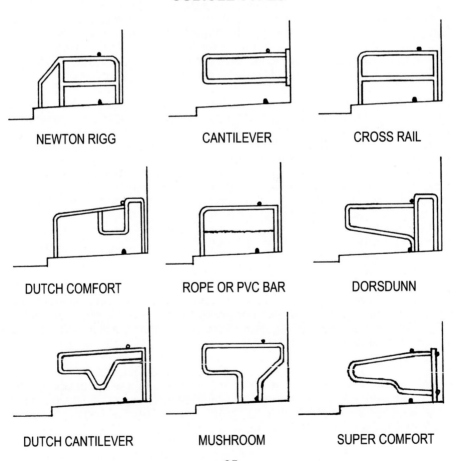

NEWTON RIGG   CANTILEVER   CROSS RAIL

DUTCH COMFORT   ROPE OR PVC BAR   DORSDUNN

DUTCH CANTILEVER   MUSHROOM   SUPER COMFORT

3.3.8 Milking Facilities

Cows will need to be milked at least twice a day (sometimes three times depending on the system employed). Therefore, it is vital for cows to have good access to and from the milking facilities, in particular when cows have to access the facilities from grazing. In general, milking should not take longer than between 2 or 3 hours each time.

Facilities should be sized to allow for variations in milk yield, the number of cows to be milked each day, the number of staff available to complete the milking and the time allowed to complete the milking of the herd. Also, do not forget to allow sufficient space for essential equipment i.e. a bulk milk tank, refrigeration gear, washing, water heating and storage etc. Note also, where the herd access the milking facilities from grazing in the summer months will influence the position, layout and size of the facilities. Allow good, bio-secure, access for large tanker lorries to get to and from the bulk milk tank.

There are many types of milking parlour commercially available. Cows can be milked in groups, as a herd, or individually (i.e. in an automatic milking machine (AMS)). However, the most common type of milking parlour has a herringbone layout, whereas large herds may be milked in a single, large rotary parlour. Clearly the building requirements vary considerably and detailed design requirements should be sought from manufacturers as appropriate.

Cows to be milked are generally moved into a collecting yard before milking. This should be big enough to accommodate the group/herd as necessary. Allow between 1.2m² and 1.5m² per cow in the collecting yard depending on breed and numbers involved. Also allow for tractor access and slurry removal. Allow between 1.5m² and 1.8m² per cow in the dispersal area, where the cows are confined within a building prior to return to their housing or grazing. A collecting yard has to adjoin the milking parlour and may have to comply with the detailed requirements of the Milk and Dairies Act for food safety reasons. The exit route from the milking parlour is often a convenient place to position a handling system, a foot bath and perhaps veterinary facilities i.e. artificial insemination (AI) facilities and calving boxes.

3.3.9 Environmental requirements

These will vary throughout the year, from building to building and can even vary between day and night. Detailed design considerations are given in Section (3.2). Well designed natural ventilation inlets and outlets are likely to be able to provide an optimum environment in the cow housing and milking facilities.

However, there may be times, particularly if cows are housed in the summer months, when they will benefit from forced air movement in the building. This is typically achieved by using mechanical ventilation systems, for example: suspending large fans at intervals along the length of the building to provide air movement in and around the stock.

3.3.10 Calving/Isolation Pens

In order to produce milk, a cow has to produce a calf, therefore, appropriate facilities will need to be provided on the dairy unit. These are sometimes called 'Loose Boxes' or 'Isolation Pens', however, isolation pens, if this is their function, should be isolated from other livestock areas of the unit, by a reasonable distance, or other appropriate means, in accordance with the bio-security policy of the dairy unit.

The number of calving boxes that will be needed depends on the number of cows in the herd and the calving pattern i.e. over how many months cows will be calving. In general, allow up to 1 per 20 cows (i.e. 5%). Siting, in general, should be adjacent to animal movement routes, so that animals needing attention can easily be diverted into a vacant box. Logically, this might be on the return route from the milking parlour where cows are closely observed on a daily basis. Calving boxes in this position, also allows easy access to the milking facilities, once the calf has had its mothers collostrum.

The design should allow for a stockman to assist with the calving (typically from behind the cow) if necessary. The minimum space required is 12m², although with the large cows of today, it may be prudent to provide up to 15m². There should be good tractor access. Each pen should be easy to clean and disinfect, should contain a separate water trough and feed trough as necessary, a sealed drainage system (to reduce the risk of disease spread), as well as access to lifting gear and other calving aids.

3.4 Buildings for Sheep

Site selection for a new building will need to consider; access roads; proximity to the shepherd; location and type of feed store; proximity to grazing and handling facilities; the direction of prevailing wind and any natural shelter; and, availability of essential services i.e. water and electricity.

The above are not listed in any particular order of importance. However, a use of an existing building that lends itself to conversion or adaptation may prove a more cost effective solution.

There are three main types of sheep housing: a) open yards; b) partly covered yards; and, c) fully enclosed buildings. Each will have merits or disadvantages over each other, but cost, flexibility, ease of use and site constraints will be major determining factors, as well as personal preference which will probably be uppermost in most shepherds' minds.

The floor surface need not be concrete and is very often rammed soil or hardcore. Areas with a high water table which are likely to get water logged should be avoided, as should very stony sites, where both could create potential foot problems. In addition soil or hardcore floors are not recommended where there is potential risk of polluting a watercourse. A concrete floor will be very expensive but will assist with day to day management and cleaning out and may also help provide an alternative use for a building. Alternatively, slats (timber, metal mesh or concrete) have been used with some success, but they are not suitable for newly born and young lambs. However, slats do require managing to prevent clogging with wool or feed; however, they may only need to be completely cleaned out every other year.

Space allowance will vary from between breeds and age, as well as whether the ewes are fully fleeced. Adequate space for tractor access and feeding or bedding down is recommended and there should be enough space (maybe in a separate building) to form lambing pens at a rate of 1 per 6 to 12 ewes, depending on the lambing period, the breed and the numbers of ewes.

Note: Where sheep are housed fully fleeced, it is vitally important to provide plenty of natural ventilation in the building, particularly where a plastic polytunnel is used to provide the accommodation, as the sheep are almost certain to suffer from heat stress.

3.4.1 Table 27: Recommended space allowances for ewes and lambs

Type and Weight (kg)	Bedded Area (m²)	Slatted Area (m²)
Pregnant Ewes 45 - 60 61 - 75 76 - 90	1.0 1.2 1.4	0.8 0.9 1.1
Ewes with lambs up to 6wks old 45 65 90	1.8 2.0 2.2	NOT RECOMMENDED
Separate creep area for lambs Up to 2 weeks old Up to 4 weeks old	0.2 0.4	NOT RECOMMENDED
Lambs up to 12 weeks old	0.5 - 0.6	NOT RECOMMENDED
Lambs and Sheep from 12 weeks to 12 months	0.75 - 0.90	0.65 - 0.8
Lambing Pen With (2?) Lambs	1.5 2.0	NOT RECOMMENDED
Rams	1.5 - 2.0	NOT RECOMMENDED

NB: Groups of ewes should be 50 or less. Where ewes are clipped prior to housing space allowances shown above may be reduced by 10%.

3.4.2 Feeding and Watering

It is very important to provide sufficient trough space for all ewes to feed at the same time, especially when feeding concentrates. This will reduce stress at feeding times and should avoid ewes trampling one another, or their lambs, when they are kept in the same pen. To facilitate this, pen layout should ideally be long and thin (probably only 3.0m wide) so that the sheep are only fed on the one side of the pen. Where more rectangular pens are used, dividing them with two sided walk-through troughs could achieve the same end. Alternatively, where appropriate, concentrates can be fed to the sheep by distributing them on top of the bedding thereby reducing the need for a trough.

3.4.3 Table 28: Recommended trough length allowances for ewes and lambs

Type and Weight (kg)	Concentrates (mm)	Ad- lib Hay or Silage (mm)
Pregnant Ewes 45 - 60 61 - 75 76 - 90 Where restricted access	 420 460 500 Not Recommended	 175 200 225 300
Ewes with lambs up to 6wks old 45 65 90 Where restricted access	 420 460 500 Not Recommended	 175 200 225 300
Separate creep area for lambs Up to 6 weeks old Over 6 weeks old Where restricted access		 50 100 300
Hoggs 20 - 30 31 - 40 41 - 50	 300 350 400	 125 150 175

NB: Where shorn ewes are housed trough lengths may be reduced by 10%. Where feeding concentrates in the same trough as forage, the length allowance for concentrates takes precedence, even in restricted feeding systems.

Clearly water troughs for sheep are much smaller than those for cattle and will need to be positioned nearer floor level. Provide separate troughs or bowls in lambing pens as appropriate. Allow up to 4.5 litres per sheep per day. Hill sheep may prefer to drink from running water and where practical this can be achieved by installing rain water guttering along one side of the pen and allowing a tap to continually, albeit slowly, run into it, thereby maintaining a flow of fresh water.

Big bale forage may be fed in specially designed feeders for sheep. Where feeding hay in a rack, they should not be positioned so high that seeds and bits of hay drop into the stocks eyes.

3.4.4 Handling facilities

Well designed handling facilities are an essential aid to management of the sheep flock. Assuming they are appropriately positioned and are of sufficient size etc, they will aid the day to day management and welfare of the flock, particularly when bringing stock on to the unit, at housing or shearing times, or when they need dipping or other treatment.

Handling facilities should ideally be positioned on slightly sloping ground as sheep tend to run better up slight inclines, towards an open horizon and away from buildings. As a general rule, allow at least $0.5m^2$ per ewe in the collecting pen and multiply this area by 3 to provide sufficient space for drying, drafting and holding areas. Therefore, the more sheep there are to be handled at any one time will determine the size of unit required. There are completely portable units/systems available that can provide a lower cost option. However, avoid sites where there is a risk of causing pollution. The main working areas of a permanent handling facility may be covered with a simple mono-pitch structure to provide shelter for the shepherd and possibly some shade from direct sun light for the sheep.

Where dipping or foot treatment facilities are included ensure adequate water supply and avoid the possibility of pollution from spillages and when disposing of the used liquids.

3.4.5 Sheep Dairying

Where sheep flocks are kept on a farm for milk production, the same principles of design, siting and layout of facilities, as considered when looking at cow milking, should be applied to the design etc. of the sheep unit as a whole. However, obviously, in a sheep milking unit the size of everything may be significantly different to that of a cow dairy unit, but the designer will still need to consider stock flow, wastes, feeding, lorry access, pollution etc. Equally the designer should bear in mind that the unit will be a food producing place and, therefore, high levels of hygiene will be required. However, in this case the Milk and Dairies Regulations do not apply, but the Food Safety Act 1990, which will be administered by the Environmental Health Department of the Local Authority, will have to be complied with.

3.5 Buildings for Calves

Under current Welfare Regulations, a calf is defined as a bovine animal up to 6 months of age. Accommodation should comply with the Welfare Code for Cattle and the Welfare of Farmed Animals (England) Regulations 2007.

Successful calf rearing relies on providing appropriate accommodation that gives each calf a dry, well bedded lying area; adequate ventilation that is draught free, particularly at stock level, at the same time as providing a minimum air volume per calf; and, adequate space for each calf to grow and thrive. These requirements should also be combined with a high level of management.

For natural ventilation design, see Section 3.2

3.5.1 Table 29: Air volume required per calf

Calf Liveweight (kg)	Air volume required (m³/head)
Up to 60	6
61 to 85	10
86 to 140	13
141 to 200	15

Note; the total number of calves in any one airspace should be limited to a maximum of around 40, or less, to assist in maintaining an appropriate environment for the calves and, in particular, help avoid respiratory problems.

3.5.2 Accommodation

Calves cannot be confined in individual stalls or pens after they are 8 weeks old, unless authorised by veterinary surgeon.

Individual pens must be at least equal to the height of the calf at the withers and the length must be at least equal to the body length of the calf, multiplied by 1.1. The table below provides a range of commercially available individual pens that may satisfy the above requirements.

3.5.3 Table 30: Typical individual calf pen sizes

Calf Liveweight (kg)	Clear Pen Length (mm)	Clear Pen Width (mm)
Up to 60	1500	750
61 to 80	1800	1000

Regulations also require that the walls of the pens should be perforated which allows each calf to have direct visual and tactile contact with other calves.

All calves must be provided with appropriate bedding. In pens it is vital that this is clean, dry and comfortable at all times. To achieve this, the pens should have a floor below the bedding that aids free drainage, i.e. a slope of 1 in 20 under the bedding; or, where the pens have slatted floor in them, bedding must be placed on top of the slats.

3.5.4 Group housing

After 8 weeks of age, all calves must be group housed. To assist management and reduce disease risk, groups should not be any bigger than 20 head and should contain animals of the same sex and age. At all times the calves must be able to stand up, turn around, lie down, rest and groom themselves without hindrance. To achieve this in group housing, the minimum unobstructed space allowance for each calf must be as indicated in the table below (or check QA requirements).

3.5.5 Table 31: Unobstructed floor space per calf

Calf Liveweight (kg)	Minimum space for each calf (m²)
Up to 150	1.5
151 to 200	2.0
Over 201	3.0

3.5.6 Feeding and Drinking

It is recommended that a completely separate area close to the calf accommodation (particularly individual pens) is provided for feed preparation. Calves housed in individual pens will usually be provided feed and water in buckets which are positioned at the front of the pens so that the calf can access them as required. All buckets must be filled at least twice a day and cleaned at least daily. Passageways between two rows of calf pens (i.e. facing each other) should be at least 1.2m wide, measured between the buckets.

Where calves are fed forage and other fibrous material, at a barrier, they should be allowed a minimum of 300mm trough space per calf, up to 200kg live weight. The need for tractor access and scraping the feed stance should be considered at the design stage and sufficient space allowed for this in the building dimensions.

Where calves are fed using an automatic feeding system, typically an ad libitum milk machine, and the distance from the machine to the teats should be as short as possible. The calves should stand on a concrete area which is free draining and, depending on group size; there should be sufficient teats for to allow each calf sufficient time to feed. Where calves do not have continuous access to the automatic feeding system, each calf should be given access to their food at the same time as other calves in the group.

3.6 Buildings for Beef Cattle and Suckler Cows

Sufficient space, good feed access, generous ventilation, effective bedding and a good water supply are the key ingredients for success in beef housing. These ensure the best possible animal welfare, health and performance. Beef buildings should have sufficient flexibility to accommodate different groups of stock of different size. Small groups of cattle are easier to manage than large ones and show less individual performance variation. Steers and heifers should generally be kept in groups of less than 40, and bulls in groups of less than 20. As far as possible, groups should be matched for size as well as sex.

Providing sufficient lying, loafing and feeding space is a key factor. The tables below can be used as a guide to minimum areas, particularly for groups of animals. Farmers need to check that the areas given against compliance standard, including organic. For practical purposes, at least 20% should be added to the minimum space allowances given, to cater for variations in cattle size, extended housing periods, and other circumstances.

3.6.1 Ensuring sufficient size

3.6.1.1 Table 32: Recommended minimum dimensions for individual calf pens (up to 8 weeks). BS5502, Part 40, 2005

Liveweight (kg)	Approx age (weeks)	Pen size (mm) length	width
Up to 60	Up to 4	1500	1000
Up to 80	Up to 8	1800	1000

3.6.1.2 Table 33: Recommended minimum space allowances for group-housed calves. DEFRA, 2003

Liveweight (kg)	Approx age (months)	Pen area (m²/head)
Up to 150	4	1.5
150 to 200	5	2.0
Over 200	7	3.0

3.6.1.3 Table 34: Recommended minimum space allowances for beef cattle on solid floors. BS5502, part 40, 2005

Liveweight (kg)	Approx age (months)	Total area (lying and feeding) (m²/head)
200	7	3.0
300	12	3.6
400	16	4.2
500	20	4.6
600	26	5.1
700	26+	5.4

3.6.1.4 Table 35: Bedded area allowance for single suckler cow and calf (excluding creep area). BS5502, part 40

Liveweight (kg)	Bedded area (lying and feeding) (m²/head)
Up to 500	5.0
Up to 600	6.0
Over 600	6.5

3.6.1.5 Table 36: Recommended minimum space allowance for growing & finishing cattle on slats, excluding trough. BS5502, part 40, 2005

Liveweight (kg)	Approx age (months)	Floor area (m²/head)
200	7	1.1
300	12	1.5
400	16	1.8
500	20	2.1
600	26	2.3
700	26+	2.5

3.6.1.6 Table 37: Minimum dimensions of cubicles for suckler cows. BS5502, part 40, 2005

Mass of cow (kg)	Length of bed with lunging space (m)	Length of bed without lunging space (m)	Clear width between divisions (m)
500	2.05	2.35	1.12
600	2.15	2.40	1.15
700	2.20	2.50	1.18
800	2.25	2.55	1.20

3.6.1.7 Table 38: Recommended minimum space allowance for cattle in woodchip corrals.

As a guide, use about double the pen area of traditional roofed bedded yards, excluding any feed stance.

Liveweight (kg)	Approx age (months)	Floor area (m²/head)
300	12	7
450	18	8
600	26	9

3.6.2 Ensuring good feed access

Make sure that all animals have ready access to feed, and that feed is not wasted by poor barrier or trough design. Keep feed covered to avoid a drop in intake and performance. It is better that all cattle can access the feed at the same time, so encouraging shy animals to feed. If access to feed is restricted, it is advisable to provide at least half the full access space, otherwise cattle can get bullied, and it will be difficult to keep feed presented in front of stock.

3.6.2.1 Table 39: Recommended clear feeding face for cattle eating simultaneously. BS5502, Part 40, 2005

Liveweight (kg)	Approx age (months)	Minimum trough space (mm/head)
200	7	400
300	12	500
400	16	550
500	20	600
600	26	670
700	26+	700
Over 800	26+	750

3.6.3 Ensuring generous ventilation

Generous ventilation is essential for good cattle performance. Apart from encouraging the spread of respiratory disease, poor ventilation leads to a more rapid deterioration of buildings, and increases bedding requirements. Under UK conditions, there is no risk of high ventilation rates causing temperatures to fall low enough to affect cattle performance. Never attempt to keep stock buildings warm by manipulating the ventilation inlets or outlets. Overstocking, water leakage and poor bedding can lead to respiratory problems, even within a well-ventilated building.

Good stock buildings allow air to be drawn easily from the eaves up to an open ridge by natural ventilation or the 'stack effect'. To work well the inlet area needs to be at least double the outlet area at the ridge. As a guide, 100 large, mature beef cattle need about 10m² of total outlet area in the ridge, with at least 20m² of inlet, preferably 40m² of inlet at the sides. Buildings with an eaves height of greater than 3.5m, with steep pitched roofs, ventilate better than low buildings with flattish roofs, which should never be used for livestock.

Umbrella buildings that have no walls or gable ends provide ideal ventilation, but they need to have at least 1.2m roof overhang to protect feed troughs filled from an outside roadway. Deep bedded cattle yards can work equally well, with cattle having access to outside yards for feeding. Such free air movement can however be compromised by siting buildings too closely together, or adding lean-to's.

Many techniques can be used to improve the ventilation of buildings, ranging from raising roof sheets on battens, opening ridges, slotting roofs, fixing side curtains and providing fans. Normally it is an inadequate ridge opening which is the cause of poor ventilation. Opening up the ridge will allow stale air to escape quickly, to be replaced by fresh air via side and gable end inlets.

3.6.3.1 Table 40: Minimum airspace for housed calves. BS5502, Part 40, 2005

Liveweight (kg)	Minimum airspace per head (m³)
Up to 60	6
60 - 85	10
85 - 140	13
140 - 200	15

3.6.4 Ensuring effective bedding

The Hillsborough Research Institute has demonstrated no significant difference in animal performance, or meat-eating quality, in cattle finished from a wide range of housing types. These include straw-bedded yards, concrete slats, and slats covered with rubber mats. Slats work well, and keep cattle clean, as long as correct stocking densities are maintained.

As a general rule, cattle finished in straw yards over a six month winter need at least 1 tonne of straw bedding per head, with bedding requirements greater on silage and root based diets, compared to hay or haylage feeding. Straw choppers and blowers will reduce the labour involved in bedding cattle, and save costs by reducing straw usage. Straw can also be saved by providing a scraped feed stance at least 3 m wide, with a kerb to prevent slurry being trampled into the bedding. This stance could save up to a third in straw bedding.

Cubicles should ideally be designed for female stock - preferably suckler cows, bulling and maiden heifers and finishing heifers. They should not be used for steers, because urine deposits halfway up the cubicle bed can cause health and hygiene problems. Many traditional covered straw yards can be converted relatively cheaply into cubicle housing. This can save substantially on straw bedding, allowing the straw to be used as part of the feed ration.

A large number of woodchip corrals have been constructed in the UK, mainly to allow suckler cows to be 'housed outside' to save on bedding costs, reduce stocking densities in yards and provide scope for rearing or finishing weaned calves, previously sold as strong stores. Open woodchip corrals work best on a free draining, sunny sites away from watercourses. Large woodchips are required 60-80 mm square, 20 mm thick, laid to a minimum depth of 300 mm. Corrals can also be used successfully for growing cattle, but finishing cattle need a period indoors on bedding to be clean enough for sale.

3.6.5 Ensuring clean water

An unlimited supply of clean drinking water is essential for good cattle performance.

At 9 months of age cattle consume about 15 litres of water daily. At 18 months they consume about 25 litres of water per day. Cattle must have easy access to water troughs, which are preferable to bowls, since they allow more cattle to drink in quick succession. Raised water troughs allow different ages of cattle to drink freely, and prevent dung contamination of the drinking water. To prevent bedding contamination, troughs should ideally be sited so that cattle can access them when they are standing on a concrete feed apron. Water troughs and bowls should be checked daily, to see if they are dispensing water.

3.6.6 Keeping Cattle Clean

To avoid charges of £20-30/head for belly clipping cattle at the lairage, it is essential to present animals for slaughter in an acceptably clean condition.

Dirty cattle cost money due to rejected animals, slower line speeds, and damages hides due to dung or careless clipping. A guide on 'clean beef cattle for slaughter' is available from the Food Standards Agency, (Food Standards Agency, 2004).

3.6.7 Safe Handling and Housing

Every farm which rears cattle should have properly designed pens and handling facilities, which are maintained in good working order. Efficient penning and handling increase profitability, by easing treatment, so ensuring healthy stock and the effective use of labour. A guide on the safe handling and housing of cattle is available from the Health and Safety Executive, (HSE, 2004).

3.7 Other Livestock

3.7.1 Pigs

3.7.1.1 Siting and Layout

Try to site well away from non-agricultural dwellings. Ensure that there is a good access. Select a dry site which is sheltered and is not visually obtrusive. Ensure that there is adequate land close by for the manure disposal without creating a pollution risk. Site well away from any coastal or inland waterway.

3.7.1.2 Basic data

Feeding can be continuous with unrestricted access, otherwise all pigs in the group should be able to feed at the same time and the space must be in addition to the floor area.

Good ventilation is required to remove or dilute aerial contamination, excess heat and moisture. In cool conditions it must also be capable of balancing heat input (animal body heat) with the heat loss through the building structure. Carbon dioxide must not rise above 0.3%. Temperature should not exceed 28°C. Humidity should not exceed 80% to limit the life of airborne bacteria. See Table 41.

Farrowing pens, with facilities to protect the piglet, should be provided. Where the sow is contained by rails the minimum unobstructed lying area should not be less than 2.1m x 0.75m plus a clear space 0.30m around the confining rails. Piglet creeps are needed to provide a warmer environment than the sow requires.

3.7.1.3 Table 41: Environmental conditions for pigs

Stock	Mass of animal up to (kg)	Group size	Type of floor	Critical air temperature		Ventilation rate per pig		Max. air speed in winter (m/s)
				Lower °C	Upper °C	Min. m³/h	Max. m³/h	
Dry sows	140	1	Concrete	21	35	14	70	0.25
		5	Concrete slats	20	33	14	90	0.25
		5	Concrete	17	32	14	100	0.25
		5	Straw	13	30	14	120	0.25
Farrowing sows	140	1	Concrete	14	32	20	135	0.25
		1	Perforated metal	12	29	20	230	0.25
		1	Straw	7	27	20	420	0.25
Young pigs	1.5	10	Concrete	24	34	1	5	Still air
		10	Straw	16	24.5	1	148	Still air
	10	10	Concrete	21	32	3	20	Still air
		10	Perforated metal	19	28	3	40	Still air
		10	Straw	14	26	3	105	Still air

Growing pigs							
20	15	Concrete	15	30	5	45	Still air
	15	Perforated metal	16	28	5	75	Still air
	15	Straw	11	25	5	430	Still air
40	15	Concrete slats	12	27	8	165	0.25
	15	Concrete	14	28	8	120	0.25
	15	Perforated metal	16	28	8	100	0.25
	15	Straw	7	25	8	325	0.25
60	15	Concrete slats	10	26	10.5	255	0.25
	15	Concrete	12	27	10.5	185	0.25
	15	Perforated metal	14	28	10.5	135	0.25
	15	Straw	7	25	10.5	535	0.25
80	15	Concrete slats	12	28	11.5	160	0.25
	15	Concrete	14	28	11.5	135	0.25
	15	Straw	9	27	11.5	215	0.25
100	15	Concrete slats	11	28	13	180	0.25
	15	Concrete	13	28	13	155	0.25
	15	Straw	8	27	13	235	0.25

NOTE: No interpolation is permitted between the masses or the stages given

112

Boar accommodation should provide individual pens. Service spacing can be within the pen or as separate penning. A minimum floor area of 7.5 m2 per boar is required with a minimum pen dimension of 2.1m. Boars should be able to see other breeding stock, particularly the sows. Service pens should be 10 m2 with minimum pen dimensions of 2.5 m.

Additionally appropriately designed pens should be provided for isolation, quarantine and sick animals needs; sited away from the main unit and access routes.

3.7.1.4 Construction data

Roofs - If to be coloured a light solar reflective colour should be used.

Walls - Should be damp proof, capable of being cleaned, disinfected, withstand knowing and lateral pressure imposed by the pig, labour and equipment

Floors - May be solid, slatted, perforated or mesh. The latter three should comply with BS 5502 part 51. Must be dry warm and easily cleaned. The sub-base of rammed hardcore 100 mm thick should be covered with a light weight no-fines concrete 100 mm thick (20 mm particle size topped with a 20 mm thick screed of 13 cement mix or 3 mm thick (SBR) latex finish. Alternatively the sub-base as described above can be covered with a 75 mm thick concrete blinding layer, a 1000 gauge poly thene DPC, light weight concrete blocks, 100 mm thick and fin ished with a 40 mm screed topping using a 1:3 mix

Insulation - The above components of the building should be insulated to the levels set out in table B.19 and the environmental conditions in table B.17

3.7.1.5 Table 42: Maximum thermal transmittance values

Recommended maximum thermal transmittance U-value of pig building structural components		
Building component	Heated buildings W/m²K	Unheated buildings
Roof Walls	0.5 0.5	0.6 0.6
Floor	Floors adjacent to (i.e. within 1 m) of perimeter walls should provide thermal transmittance values comparable with the adjacent wall, elsewhere a value of 1.	

Pen walls - For farrowing houses: 0.4m high.
For weaner per division: 0.6m high on a flat deck system.
For finishers: 1.0-1.2 high

Boar pen walls should be solid with a height of 1.75m. In large pens fencing partitions can be used. In this case all rails should be vertical; no horizontal framing rails should have a gap of more than 40mm from the floor surface.

Pen doors - Must open outwards

Ventilation - Any automatic ventilation must have fail safe facilities. In the event of a breakdown due to a fault in the system or a power cut an alarm should be set off and if no automatically switched standby generator is avail

3.7.1.6 Table 43: Maximum allowable gas concentrations in occupied buildings

Maximum allowable gas concentrations in occupied buildings in parts per million (p.p.m)	
Gas	Allowable concentration
Carbon dioxide Carbon monoxide Ammonia Hydrogen sulphide	3000 10 20 5

Water - Drinkers should be located in dunging areas to avoid wetting the lying area.

Drainage - Is influenced by the housing system. Dry beds are essential and porous or drained surfaces under straw bedding should be considered. A fall of 1:40 should be provided where there is a separate drainage for urine and washings. Level floors below slats of all types and scraped passages.

3.7.1.7 Weighing and handling facilities

Most housing is arranged so that either dunging or feeding passages can be used for weighing, by the introduction of a portable weighing crate, for treatment. For larger units a specialist race should be provided and loading facilities with controlled access from all sections of the housing. Washing, weighing and treatment areas should be enclosed and provided with water, electricity and drainage.

3.7.1.8 Regulations

Under the 'Welfare of Farmed Animals (England) (Amendment) Regulations 2000 & 2003 the following issues are relevant:

- Materials used for the construction of accommodation, and, in particular for the construction of pens, cages, stalls and equipment with which animals may come into contact, shall not be harmful to them and shall be capable of being thoroughly cleaned and disinfected.

- Accommodation and fittings for securing animals shall be constructed and maintained so that there are no sharp edges or protrusions likely to cause injury to them.

- The internal surfaces of housing and pens should be made of materials that you can easily clean and disinfect regularly, and easily replace when necessary.

- If you are going to treat these surfaces, use paints or wood preservatives that are safe to use with animals. There is a risk of lead poisoning from old paintwork, especially if you use second-hand building materials.

- Floors: Where pigs are kept in a building, floors shall

  o Be smooth but not slippery so as to prevent injury to the pigs;
  o Be so designed, constructed and maintained as not to cause injury or suffering to pigs standing or lying on them;
  o Be suitable for the size and weight of the pigs; and
  o Where no litter is provided, form a rigid, even and stable surface.

- When concrete slatted floors are used for pigs kept in groups, the maximum width of the openings must be:

  o 11 mm for piglets;
  o 14 mm for weaners;
  o 18 mm for rearing pigs;
  o 20 mm for gilts after service and sows.

The minimum slat width must be:

  o 50 mm for piglets and weaners;
  o 80 mm for rearing pigs, gilts after service and sows.

- Good floor design and adequate maintenance is essential. Poorly constructed floors, slats that are not properly matched to the weight/size of pig and surfaces that are worn and/or damaged, can cause injury to the feet and legs of pigs. Excessive gaps should be avoided as they can trap thefeet/claws and may cause physical damage. Damaged floors must be repaired immediately.

- Where bedding is provided, this must be clean, dry and not harmful to the pigs.

- The lying area should always be kept dry and pen floors, including the dunging area, should be drained effectively. Where bedding is provided, this must be clean and dry, regularly topped up or changed, and not detrimental to the health of the pigs.
- You should avoid wide or abrupt fluctuations in temperature in housing systems within any 24-hour period. Wide fluctuations in the daily temperature regime can create stress that may trigger outbreaks of vice, such as tail biting, or disease such as pneumonia. You should maintain a higher than normal level of vigilance at these times.
- When pigs are moved to new accommodation, the possibility of cold stress occurring as a result of sudden changes in the thermal environment should be reduced. This can be done by ensuring that the pen is dry, by thprovision of bedding, such as straw, or by preheating the building.
- When you are removing slurry from under slats, you must take special care to avoid fouling the air with dangerous gases (such as ammonia), which can kill both humans and animals. Buildings should either be empty of very well ventilated during this procedure.

3.7.1.9 Table 44: Temperature requirements

Category of Pig	Temperature (°C)
Sows	15-20
Suckling pigs in creeps	25-30
Weaned pigs (3-4 weeks)	27-32
Later weaned pigs (5 weeks +)	22-27
Finishing pigs (porkers)	15-21
Finishing pigs (baconers)	13-18

3.7.1.10 Lighting and Noise levels

Where animals are kept in a building, adequate lighting (whether fixed or portable) shall be available to enable them to be thoroughly inspected at any time.

Animals kept in buildings shall not be kept without an appropriate period of rest from artificial lighting.

Where pigs are kept in an artificially lit building then lighting with an intensity of at least 40 lux shall be provided for a minimum period of 8 hours per day subject to paragraph 16 of Schedule 1 to these regulations.

Pigs shall not be exposed to constant or sudden noise. Noise levels above 85 dBA shall be avoided in that part of any building where pigs are kept.

116

You should have enough fixed or portable lighting available at any time if you need to inspect any animals, for example, during farrowing.

The siting of machinery such as feed milling units should be appropriate to minimise the noise impact on housed stock. Any bell or buzzer which is likely to occur erratically, for example, a visitor to the site, should be sufficiently loud to attract human attention but without causing undue alarm to the stock.

Where pigs are fed on a rationed feed level to control intake, you should ensure that adequate trough space is provided to ensure that all pigs can receive their allocation. The following guidelines for trough space per pig apply:

3.7.1.11 Table 45: Trough space requirements

Weight of pig (kg)	Trough space (cm)
5	10
10	13
15	15
35	20
60	23
90	28
120	30

(DEFRA, 2003)

Good hygiene is necessary for storage and feeding systems as moulds can develop in stale feed which can have a detrimental effect on pigs. Feed bins should be cleaned out regularly.

All pigs over two weeks of age must have permanent access to a sufficient quantity of fresh drinking water.

3.7.1.12 Feed and water

There are several factors you should take into consideration when looking at the provision of water to pigs:

- the total volume available;
- the flow rate (pigs will not spend a long time taking water);
- the method of provision e.g. the type of drinker; and its accessibility to all stock.

3.7.1.13 Table 46: Guide to minimum daily water requirements for various weights of pig

Weight of pig (kg)	Daily requirement (litres)	Minimum flow rate through nipple drinkers (litres/min)
Newly weaned	1.0 - 1.5	0.3
Up to 20 kgs	1.5 - 2.0	0.5 - 1.0
20 kgs - 40 kgs	2.0 - 5.0	1.0 - 1.5
Finishing pigs up to 100 kgs	5.0 - 6.0	1.0 - 1.5
Sows and gilts - pre-service and in-pig	5.0 - 8.0	2.0
Sows and gilts - in lactation	15 - 30	2.0
Boars	5.0 - 8.0	2.0

(DEFRA, 2003)

Waste water and excessive flow rates can be detrimental, particularly for sows in farrowing accommodation and very young pigs.

You should carefully consider the height at which water nipples and bowls are placed. All pigs must be able to access the drinking point. This might require height-adjustable, or several different, drinkers at various heights when groups of pigs or a range of weights are housed together or when pigs are housed in a pen for a long period.

Where nipple drinkers are used, a drinking point should be available for each ten pigs on rationed feeding. On unrestricted feeding, one nipple drinker should provide adequate supply for 15 pigs given sufficient flow rates. Where trough systems are used, the following guidelines should be applied:

3.7.1.14 Table 47: Trough space requirements according to weight of pig

Weight of pig (kg)	Trough space per head (cm)
Up to 15	0.8
15 - 35	1.0

(DEFRA, 2003)

If you use a wet feeding system, pigs must have access to a separate fresh water supply.

Feed and water should not be completely withdrawn from sows which are being dried off.

3.7.1.15 Weaners and rearing pigs

The unobstructed floor area available to each weaner or rearing pig reared in a group shall be at least:

- 0.15 m2 for each pig where the average weight of the pigs in the group is 10 kg or less;

- 0.20 m2 for each pig where the average weight of the pigs in the group is more than 10 kg but less than or equal to 20 kg;

- 0.30 m2 for each pig where the average weight of the pigs in the group is more than 30 kg but less than or equal to 50 kg;

- 0.55 m2 for each pig where the average weight of the pigs in the group is more than 50 kg but less than or equal to 85 kg;

- 0.65 m2 for each pig where the average weight of the pigs in the group is more than 85 kg but less than or equal to 110 kg;

- 1.00 m2 for each pig where the average weight of the pigs in the group is more than 110 kg.

The figures above are minimum requirements; the type of housing and its management may mean that greater space allowances are necessary. The total floor space should be adequate for sleeping, feeding and exercising. The lying area, excluding the dunging and exercise areas, should be of sufficient size to allow all the pigs to lie down on their sides at the same time.

3.7.1.16 Dry sows and gilts

Sows and gilts shall be kept in groups except during the period between seven days before the predicted day of farrowing and the day on which the weaning of piglets (including any piglets fostered) is complete.

The pen where the group is kept must have sides greater than 2.8 m in length, except where there are less than 6 individuals in the group, when the sides of the pen must be no less than 2.4 m in length.

The total unobstructed floor area available to each gilt after service and to each sow when gilts and /or sows are kept in groups must be at least 1.64 m2 and 2.25 m2 respectively. When these animals are kept in groups of less than 6 individuals the unobstructed floor area must be increased by 10%. When these animals are kept in groups of 40 or more individuals the unobstructed floor area may be decreased by 10%.

For gilts after service and pregnant sows a part of the area required in previous paragraph equal to at least 0.95 m2 per gilt and 1.3 m2 per sow must be of continuous solid floor of which a maximum of 15% is reserved for drainage openings.

3.7.2 Poultry Housing - Laying hens

3.7.2.1 Non-cage system:

1. All newly built or rebuilt non-cage systems of production for keeping laying hens and all such systems of production brought into use for the first time, shall comply with the requirements of this schedule.

2. On and after 1st January 2007, all non-cage systems of production for keeping laying hens shall also comply with the following requirements:

3. All systems must be equipped in such a way that all laying hens have:

a. Either linear feeders providing at least 10 cm per bird or circular feeders providing at least 4cm per bird; and

b. Either continuous drinking troughs providing 2.5cm per hen or circular drinking troughs providing 1 cm per hen.

And, in addition, where nipple drinkers or cups are used, there shall be at least one nipple drinker or cup for every 10 hens. Where drinking points are plumbed in, at least two cups or two nipple drinkers shall be within reach of each hen.

c. At least one nest for every seven hens. If group nests are used, there must be at least 1 m^2 of nest space for a maximum of 120 hens.

d. Perches, without sharp edges, and providing at least 15 cm per hen. Perches must not be mounted above the litter and the horizontal distance between perches must be at least 30 cm and the horizontal distance between the perch and the wall must be at least 20 cm; and

e. At least 205 cm^2 of littered area per hen, the litter occupying at least one third of the ground surface.

4. The floors of installations must be constructed so as to support each of the forward-facing claws of each bird's foot.

5. In addition to the requirements of paragraphs 2 and 3-

a. If systems are used here the laying hens can move freely between different levels-

  i. There shall be no more than four levels.

  ii. The headroom between the levels must be at least 45 cm;

iii. The drinking and feeding facilities must be distributed in such a way as to provide equal access for all hens; and

iv. The levels must be so arranged as to prevent droppings falling on levels on the levels below; and

b. If laying hens have access to open runs-

i.There must be several popholes giving direct access to the outer area, at least 35 cm high and 40 cm wide and extending along the entire length of the building; and in any case, a total opening of 2m must be available per group of 1,000 hens; and

ii. Open runs must be of an area appropriate to the stocking density and to the nature of the ground, in order to prevent any contamination, and equipped with shelter from inclement weather and predators and, of necessary, appropriate drinking troughs.

6. Subject to paragraph 7, the stocking density must not exceed nine laying hens per square metre of useable area.

7. Where on 3rd August 1999 the establishment applied a system where the usable area corresponded to the available ground surface, and the establishment is still applying this system when the Welfare of Farmed Animals (England) (Amendment) Regulations 2002 come into force, a stocking density of 12 hens per square metre is authorised until 31st December 2011.

3.7.2.2 Conventional Cages:

1. On and after 1st January 2003 all conventional (un-enriched) cage systems shall comply with the following requirements:

a. At least 550 cm2 per hen of cage area, measuring in a horizontal plane, which may be used without restriction, in particular not including non-waste deflection plates liable to restrict the area available., must be provided for each laying hen. However, where the non-waste deflection plate is places so as not to restrict the area available for the hen to use, then that area may be included in the measurement.

b. A feed trough which may be used without restriction must be provided. Its length must be at least 10 cm multiplied by the number of hens in the cage.

c. Unless nipple drinker or drinking cups are provided, each cage must have a continuous drinking channel of the same length as the feed trough mentioned in sub-paragraph (b). Where drinking points are plumbed in, at least two nipple drinkers or two cups must be within reach of each cage.

d. Cages must be at least 40 cm high over at least 65% of the cage area and not less than 35 cm at any point; the area being obtained by multiplying 550 cm2 by the number of birds kept in the cage.

e. Floors of cages must be constructed so as to support each of the for ward- facing claws of each foot of each bird. Floor slope must not exceed 14% or 8 degrees when made of rectangular wire mesh and 21.3% or 12 degrees for other types of floor; and

f. Cages shall be fitted with suitable claw-shortening devices

2. On and after 1st January 2003 no person shall build or bring into service for the first time any cage system referred to in paragraph 1 for the keeping of laying hens.

3. On and after 1st January 2012 no person shall keep any laying hen in any cage system referred to in paragraph 1.

3.7.2.3 Enriched Cages:

1. All cage systems (other than those referred to above) shall be enriched to comply with the requirements of this schedule.

2. Laying hens must have-

a. At least 750 cm2 of cage area per hen, 600 cm2 of which shall be useable; the height of the cage other than that above the useable area shall be at least 20 cm at every point and no cage shall have a total area of less than 2000 cm2

b. A nest;

c. Litter such that pecking and scratching are possible; and

d. Appropriate perches allowing at least 15 cm per hen;

3. A feed trough which may be used without restriction must be provided. Its length must be at least 12 cm multiplied by the number of hens in a cage.

4. Each cage must have a drinking system appropriate to the size of the group; where nipple drinkers are provided, at least two nipple drinkers or two cups must be within the reach of each hen.

5. To facilitate inspection, installation and depopulation of hens there must be a minimum aisle width of 90 cm between tiers of cages and a space of at least 35 cm must be allowed between the floor of the building and the bottom tier of cages.

6. Cages must be fitted with suitable claw-shortening devices.

3.7.2.4 Conditions Applicable to All Systems:

1. All hens must be inspected by the owner or the person responsible for the hens at least once a day.

2. The sound level shall be minimised. Constant or sudden noise shall be avoided. Ventilation fans, feeding machinery or other equipment shall be constructed placed, operated and maintained in such a way that they cause the least possible noise.

3. All buildings shall have light levels sufficient to allow hens to see one another and be seen clearly, to investigate their surroundings visually and to show normal levels of activity. Where there is natural light, light apertures must be arranged in such a way that light is distributed evenly within the accommodation.

After the first days of conditioning, the lighting regime shall be such as to prevent health and behavioural problems. Accordingly it must follow a 24 hour rhythm and include an adequate uninterrupted period of darkness lasting, by way of indication, about one third of the day, so that the hens may rest and to avoid problems such as immunodepression and ocular anomalies. A period of twilight of sufficient duration ought to be provided when the light is dimmed so that the hens may settle down without disturbance or injury.

4. Those parts of buildings, equipment or utensils which are in contact with the hens shall be thoroughly cleansed and disinfected regularly and in any case every time depopulation is carried out and before a new batch of hens is brought in. While the cages are occupied, the surfaces and all equipment shall be kept satisfactorily clean. Droppings must be removed as often as necessary and dead hens must be removed every day.

5. Cages must be suitably equipped to prevent hens escaping.

6. Accommodation comprising two or more tiers of cages must have devices or appropriate measures taken to allow inspection of all tiers without difficulty and facilitate the removal of hens.

7. The design and dimensions of the cage door must be such that an adult hen can be removed without undergoing unnecessary suffering or sustaining injury.

8. Subject to paragraph 9, no person shall mutilate any laying hen.

9. In order to prevent feather pecking and cannibalism, until 31st

December 2010 beak trimming of birds is permitted in all systems provided it is carried out -

a. By persons over 18 years of age;

b. On chickens that are less than 10 days old and intended for laying; and

c. In accordance with the Veterinary Surgery (Exemptions) Order 1692 (5) (2002)

3.7.3 Milking goats

Minimum herd size for a single enterprise farm - 400 milkers

3.7.3.1 Siting and layout

Access to the parlour for the goats should be via a collection yard. Its size will be dependent on group sizes but should be in easy reach of the housing. The parlour may be detached or attached to the main yard (housing) depending on site conditions. The parlour will need to be able to be closed off from the housing. The dairy should be adjacent to, but separate, to the parlour.

3.7.3.2 Basic data

There are several milking parlour layouts and configurations available. Most have cascading self-locking yokes to keep the milking goat correctly positioned during milking.

The height of the milking platform will be dependent on the operator and manufacturer but will typically be 0.9 m above the operator's pit. Parlour manufacturers will provide drawings for building work in relation to the size and configuration of parlour being installed. Commercial goat milking herds will have goats standing at right angles to the operator, as a minimum on one side but often the parlour will be "doubled up", i.e. milking units or each side of the operator's pit. Larger units are now milked in rotary parlours.

3.7.3.3 Goat milking parlour spacings

It is suggested that figures are sought from the main milking machine manufacturers.

With 90° (right angled) parlours, goats are either milked down one side with one milking unit per goat, or the parlour is doubled up, i.e. two rows of goats on either side of the operator's pit with each place having a dedicated milking unit.

With the cascade yoke system as the animals enter the parlour all but the most

distant feed place is closed off. When the lead animal puts its head into the feeder the yoke locks and opens the next feeder. This process continues until all animals are yoked.

There are other milking facility options, the most common being the rotary parlour.

3.7.3.4 Table 48: Milking parlour spacings

Floor to underside of barriers (mm)	Width of passage (mm)	Feed barrier to rump rail (mm)	Width of gap in feeder (mm)
700 - 900	260 - 400	690 - 970	120 - 160

3.7.3.5 Construction data

Building standards are as for dairy cow milking premises.

3.7.3.6 Housing

Goats are usually housed all year round, as they can be difficult to handle at grazing and are prone to parasitic infestations. They are normally loosed on straw with access to an un-strawed, concrete exercise and feeding/loafing area. The abrasive surface helps maintain foot condition.

3.7.3.7 Table 49: Goat housing space standards

Lying and exercise (m2/goat)	Manger space (m/goat)	Pen depth (m)
2.0-2.5	0.4-0.5	4.5

Ventilation, water, artificial lighting and construction standards are similar to sheep. However, all wooden surfaces should be protected up to a height of at least 2 m and all plastic water piping and electrical wiring must also be correctly protected when within reach of the animals.

To be comparable standards as for dairy cows and sized in accordance with herd numbers. Regulations concerning production methods and hygiene are controlled by the Dairy Hygiene Inspectorate Animal Health Agency.

3.7.4 Deer

Species   Red   }   main species
           Fallow }   to be farmed

3.7.4.1 Table 50: Deer weight

	Red (kg)	Fallow (kg)
Stags (mature)	140-180	90
Hinds	90-110	60-70
Yearling	80-100	40-50
Weaned calf	40-45	20-25

3.7.4.2 General

Hinds well grown will breed at 18 months of age. Fallow deer are more flighty and less adaptable to farming constraints. The Rut starts in September. Gestation period 230-235 days. Deer are not well insulated therefore they require shelter e.g. woodland or shelter belts plus supplementary feed. They can damage trees (bark stripping) and on heavy land, pasture can be severely damaged.

3.7.4.3 Access

Good access is essential for transport on and off the farm plus well designed loading facilities to minimise damage and stress.

3.7.4.4 Fencing

This is one of the major costs. Deer that escape may well become wild stock. Avoid siting fence lines on steep gradients and near hillocks (jumping out points). All paddocks should lead to handling pens without stock being disturbed in adjacent paddocks.

3.7.4.5 Table 51: Deer fencing

	Boundary	Internal
Quality	High Tensile netting	High tensile netting
Height	1.8 m	1.5 to1.8 m
Wires Horizontal	13 to 17	13 to 17
Spacings	Variable	Variable
Vertical Spacings	150 mm	300 mm Alternative high tensile wires with intermediate droppers
Straining posts diameter 225 mm Struts diameter 100 mm Straining posts at changes of direction diameter 150-200 mm Spacing up to 10 m level ground - more on undulating ground		

3.7.4.6 Electric Fences

"Hot wire" offset at chest height to reinforce boundary fences. As a feeder wire carried along the top of boundary fences for paddocks. It gives flexibility and better grassland management. High output mains units are recommended.

3.7.4.7 Handling Pens

Independent access from each paddock to reduce disturbance. Good access for out loading stock for slaughter or dispatch. The lead-in race, well fenced which is masked to give a solid appearance on approach to collecting yard. Collecting area large enough to hold all the deer to be handled at any one time, without pressure. Walls solid to 2.4 m high. Space allowance per:-

Calf	0.3 to 0.5 m2
Yearling	0.5 to 0.6 m2
Adult hind	0.5 to 0.6 m2
Adult stag	approx. 1.0 m2
(Antlers removed)	

All entry gates to be 3.6 m wide (to allow free movement).
Crush pen to hold 5-10 animals.
Crush/weigh crate entered from crush pen via swing gate or short race.
Crush of "squeeze crate" or "drop floor crush" design (animal is held by body and legs are free). Access to the animal is required from front, rear and sides.
Weigh crate - box type with animal standing freely.

All pens sides should be solid (timber planks or plywood sheets) and free from obstruction. Handling pens should be covered and light restricted to the needs of the operator for inspection. Floors should be hardcore, aggregate or deeply gravelled.

Weaned calves perform better if housed during the first winter. Adult stock may require housing on heavy land to prevent soil structure and pasture damage.

3.7.4.8 Table 52: Pen spacings

Animal	Floor space (m²)	Trough space (mm)
Weaned calf (40 kg)	2	450
Yearling (90 kg)	2.5	750
Adult hind	3.0	750
Adult stag (antlers removed)	3.0	750

3.7.4.9 Structural Requirements

Structural requirements as for sheep and young cattle.

3.7.4.10 Ventilation

Ventilation - ad-lib without draught at stock level.

3.7.4.11 Water

Water - clean and fresh as for cattle.

3.7.4.12 Pen Walls

Pen walls - minimum 2.0 m high, preferably solid.

3.7.4.13 External Walls

External walls - built to deer shoulder height, windbreak material above to eaves. Allow other farm activities to be seen; reducing vice and boredom.

3.7.4.14 Floors

Floors - hard level and well drained. If feed area is left un-bedded helps to keep feet sound.

3.7.4.15 Group Size Limits

Group size limit 10-15 animals and be prepared to remove any animals that are being bullied. Avoid projections and sharp corners - deer are livelier than other farm stock and flesh is easily damaged.

Section 4

4.1 Types of store

Crop storage buildings are classified according to the type of building and the crop stored in it.

4.1.1 Table 53: Types of building for crop storage

Type of Building		Type of Crop
A	**Storage and Conditioning**	
1	Ventilated Stores	
	(i) Bulk Stores	Potatoes, Onions, Carrots, Red Beet
	(ii) Pallet stores	Farm crops generally e.g. potatoes, vegs. Horticultural crops, e.g. vegs,
2	Cool Stores	soft fruit and flowers.
3	Controlled Atmosphere stores	Apples, pears, etc.
4	Grain Stores	Cereals, pulses and seed
B	**Processing Buildings**	
1	Packing Sheds	Vegetables, fruit and flowers
2	Chitting Houses	Seed Potatoes

4.1.2 Grain - Siting and Layout

- Near to good farm access road and adequate turning circle.

- Allow for future extensions or alternative methods of storage handling and conditioning.

- Avoid sloping sites and ground with low load bearing pressure.

4.1.3 Basic data

- All grain storage is in large parcels either in large bins or on the floor.
- Storage in bins is more flexible catering for different varieties and qualities, also lends itself to automation.
- Bins should not have a floor area greater than 3 m x 3 m.
- Floor storage is adequate for a limited number of varieties, say up to a maximum of four and more difficult to manage to achieve a high quality product.
- Grain bins and walls of floor stores must be designed in accordance with BS 5502 part 22 to cater for pressures exerted by the crops and associated handling equipment. Natural light should be eliminated as far as possible to discourage birds and other livestock and the whole store must be vermin proof. Artificial light (100-300 lux) and power is necessary for inspection, handling and drying.
- Either system of storage can be associated with any form of drying.

4.1.4 On floor grain drying

- Laterals for on floor drying 0.9 m centres. Maximum length 10 m (therefore maximum internal span of building 22 m preferably 20 m). Laterals to stop 0.5 m from external walls.
- Maximum height for drying 2.5 m - 3 m.
- Minimum airflow 0.024 m^3/s per tonne in wet areas against a static pressure of 1000 N/m^2.
- Maximum airspeed in main duct 10 m/s. Louvred outlets maximum airspeed 4 m/s.
- Heater if required 3 Kw per 0.5 m^3/s gives temperature rise of 5.5 C.

4.1.5 Bin drying (Indoor square bins)

- Airflows as for on floor drying. For air- sweep emptying 0.5 m^3/s per m^2 floor area (at 1000 N/m^2).

4.1.6 Bin Drying (Outdoor Bins - circular)

- Arrange in semi-circle or parallel lines. Total capacity 500 tonnes but commercially 2500 tonnes.

- Airflow 0.1 m^3/s per tonne over whole floor area. Heater as for on floor system. Max height for drying 3 m.

4.1.7 Conditioning

- Airflow 0.0024 m³/s per tonne or use mobile vertical augers for turning grain.

4.1.8 Drying

- The drying can be achieved by:-

- Continuous or batch driers fixed,
- Continuous or batch driers portable,
  or
- Ventilation floors and ducts.

- In the case of (c) the crop being dried must not be in layers exceeding 3 metres depth for wheat, barley and oats, 1 metre is the maximum for linseed, oil seed rape, herbage seed and denser crops. Actual storage depths can be much greater.

- After drying and placing in store a crop will start to take up moisture and gradually deteriorate, therefore all stores where crops are being held for any length of time should incorporate low-volume aeration.

4.1.9 Table 54: Weights and measures for storage

Commodity	Kg per m3	m3 per tonne
Wheat	785	1.3
Barley	705	1.4
Oats	513	1.9
Rye	705	1.4
Maize	753	1.3
Peas	785	1.3
Beans	833	1.2
Linseed	705	1.4

4.1.10 Table 55: Storage capacity in framed structures per 4.8 m bay - Level storage.

Commodity	Wheat			Barley		
m3 per tonne	1.3			1.4		
Height stored	1 m	2 m	3 m	1 m	2 m	3 m
Span in m:						
6.0	22	44	66	21	42	63
7.8	29	58	87	28	56	84
9.0	33	66	99	31	62	93
10.8	40	80	120	37	74	111
12.0	44	88	132	41	82	123
13.2	49	98	147	45	90	135
14.4	53	106	159	49	98	147

4.1.11 Table 56: Addition for heaped storage

Span in m:	Wheat	Barley
6.0	16	15
7.8	25	24
9.0	35	33
10.8	50	46
12.0	62	58
13.2	76	70
14.4	90	84

4.1.12 Table 57: On floor storage and drying - Capacity per metre span of building - Level storage, Grain and Pulses

Crop	Wheat	Barley	Oats	Beans	Peas	Maize	H. seed	Rape	Linseed
Density m³/tonne	1.3	1.4	1.9	1.8	1.3	1.3	4.0	1.6	1.4
Storage/drying depth	3	3	3	3	3	3	1*	1*	1*
Bay size 4.8 m 6.0 m	11.0 13.8	10.3 12.8	7.6 9.5	8.0 10.0	11.0 13.8	11.0 13.8	12.0 15.0	3.0 3.75	3.5 4.28
Normal 22 m span building capacity 4.8 m 6.0 m per bay	220 276	206 256	152 190	160 200	220 276	220 276	240 300	60 75	70 85

H. = Herbage

4.1.13 Table 58: Normal design criteria for on-floor storage

	Length m	X section	Air speed	Air flow m³/s/t	Spacing
Main duct (max.) Lateral duct (max.)	30 10	1.5 × 0.8 m	10 m/s 7 – 10 m/s	0.02 to 0.05	0.9
Heating	3 Kilowatts per 100 tonnes				
Outlet ventilators	4 metres per second in gable ends				
Lighting – Natural	Nil				
• Artificial	100 lux general – 300 lux point lighting and inspection				
Drainage	Internal nil – External site and stormwater only				

4.1.14 Table 59: Bin capacity for typical sizes

Length in m	Breadth in m	Height in m	Capacity per bin in tonnes			
			Wheat	Barley	Oats	Peas
3.0	3.0	9.0	63	58	43	63
3.0	3.0	6.0	42	39	39	42
3.0	3.0	3.0	21	20	20	21
3.0	2.4	7.2	40	37	37	40
3.0	2.4	4.5	25	23	23	25
2.4	2.4	6.0	27	25	25	27
2.4	2.4	3.9	18	16	16	18

4.1.15 Table 60: Capacity of barley tower silos of typical dimensions

Diameter	Height to eaves	Capacity based on 1.4m3/ tonnes at moisture content 22%
M	M	tonnes
4.42	4.42	48
4.42	5.28	58
4.42	6.29	70
4.42	7.31	80
4.42	8.33	91
4.42	9.34	102
6.10	5.28	110
6.10	6.29	131
6.10	7.31	152
6.10	8.33	173
6.10	9.34	195
6.10	12.39	258
6.10	13.41	280
6.10	14.42	301
6.10	15.44	322
6.10	16.45	343
6.10	17.47	364
6.10	18.49	386

4.1.16 Table 61: Capacity for Circular Silo Storage

Commodity	Wheat		Barley	
Diameter in m	4.5	6.0	4.5	6.0
Height in m				
3.0	37	65	34	61
4.5	55	98	51	91
6.0	73	130	68	121
7.5	92	163	85	151
9.0	110	196	102	182

4.1.17 Table 62: Capacity of typical intake pits

Dimensions of pit in metres			Capacity in tonnes	
Length A	Breadth B	Depth C	Wheat	Barley
1.8	1.5	1.8	1.2	1.1
2.4	1.8	2.1	2.3	2.1
3.0	2.4	2.7	5.0	4.6
3.6	2.7	3.3	8.2	7.6

4.1.18 Intake pits structure Diagram (Figure 6)

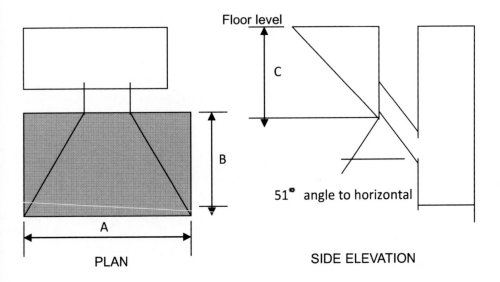

Floor level

C

B

A

51° angle to horizontal

PLAN

SIDE ELEVATION

4.1.19 Shell

Structural frame designed to take thrust of surcharged grain eaves height 4.2m-6m. Bay width 4.8m or 6m. Spans up to 22m. See section (framed structures). Building should be bird and vermin proof.

4.1.20 Floor

Reinforced concrete 150mm above ground level with damp proof membrane joined to walling. Waterproof all underground works. Timber or concrete 'drive over' slotted floors, brick floors or under floor ducts according to choice of system.

4.1.21 Walls

Reinforced mass concrete, reinforced concrete block or diaphragm brickwork. Consult a Structural Engineer. Prefabricated galvanised steel profiled panels fixed to frame stanchions and top fixing channel. Prefabricated reinforced concrete panels fixed to frame stanchions. Prefabricated timber panels with framework fixed inside stanchions. Access doorways, 4.8m-6m wide by 6m high.

4.1.22 Roof

Corrugated fibre cement, PVC coated or galvanised profiled sheet. Roof pitch 14°C -16°C

4.1.23 Towers

Steel with glass enamelling. Concrete base to exceed diameter by 600 mm.

4.1.24 Lighting

Natural should be avoided as it encourages birds. Artificial to working areas and machinery areas must be fully illuminated. Make sure 3-phase electricity is available for power. All installations in accordance with the regulations of the IEE.

4.1.25 Ventilation

Natural, particularly for dust control. Gable and wall louvers with 6 mm wire or plastic mesh either fixed or mechanically operated. Mechanical air intake according to drying or conditioning system chosen. Extractor fans may be needed. A fan house may be built on the end of the building, connected to the main air ducts.

4.1.26 Water

Standpipe with hose connections.

4.1.27 Drainage

Internal not required. External rainwater disposal to soakaway or catchpit.

4.2 Potato Storage

Very similar to grain storage (see section 4.2)

4.2.1 General storage

Potatoes can be stored in bulk or in boxes. All stores must be fully insulated regardless of storage period. The degree of insulation is described as Watts per m^2 per degree K, or C. Minimum insulation value should by 0.3 W\$m^2$K. Most modern buildings would aim to increase the insulation in the roof to 0.28 W\$m^2$K.

In box stores the side walls do not need to be load bearing while in bulk stores the walls must resist the thrust of the crop loaded to full storage height. Load bearing walls must be designed to BS5502.

All potato stores need ventilation systems with facility to air mix and re-circulate. A refrigeration and a heating source are desirable for many stores. Air heating in the roof space minimises condensation in stores with a high crop storage temperature.

The first priority is to dry the crop and remove all surface moisture. Ideally this is followed by up to 10 days curing (wound healing) at 12-15 deg C. In situations where loading takes place over more than 10 days then the priority after drying must be to cool the crop. Whenever possible, high humidity air should be used to dry and cure the crop.

      Commonly recommended storage temperatures:
Seed potatoes	3-4 °C
Table consumption	3-4 °C
French fry production	6-8 °C
Crisp production	7-10 °C

Potatoes should be maintained at a relative humidity of >95%.

4.2.2 Potato Chitting Houses

The cost of good equipment for chitting houses is more than compensated for by increased yield and uniformity of harvested sample.

Glasshouse type may need some form of heating, to encourage sprouting, and ventilation to control the rate of sprout growth. Lighting will be natural. Traditional buildings need insulation and ventilation to control sprouting. Lighting is by warm white fluorescent tubes hung vertically between double rows of seed trays spaced from 2.2 m to 4.5 m according to variety. Lighting would initially start at 8-10 hours per day increasing to 12-14 hours.

Seed trays, normally timber, 0.8 m x 0.45 m x 0.15 m and from 4-3 trays per 50 kg of seed.

Stacking should preferably be two rows per spur with pathways between. Normal 6 m eaves glasshouse allows 16 trays high at eaves and 23 in centre. For traditional buildings the heights of stack will vary.

Capacity of store (allowing for pathways) can be calculated as follows:-

Capacity in tonnes $\quad = \quad \dfrac{W \times L \times H}{X}$

W = number of rows of trays across store.
L = number of trays along store
H = number of trays stacked vertically
X = 70 where loading rate 3½ trays per 50 kg
  = 80 where loading rate 4 trays per 50 kg

Humidity should be held at 90% to 95%.

Temperature ranges controlled by ventilation and heat source 2 - 4 deg C to prevent growth of sprout.

Drop to 4° to prevent temperature shock of planting into cold soil.
7°C - 13 °C to achieve satisfactory growth rates.
13 °C - 16 °C to seal wounds when introduced to storage (10 days).
16°C - 24 °C to open large number of eyes (many small potatoes produced - seed production)

NB. Storage from harvest time until setting out in chitting trays will be in normal storage buildings with the conditions being as for general storage above.

4.2.3 Constructional data

As for grain storage except for tower silos, insulation and ventilation. See previous sections.

4.2.4 Table 63: Typical storage heights, airflow and environment

Crop	Max. storage height (m)	Spacing of ducts (m)	Typical airflow m³/s/t	Storage conditions		Max. thermal transmittance "U"	
				Temp °C	Rel. humidity	Walls W/m²K	Roofs W/m²K
Carrots	3.0	1.8	0.025 to 0.050	0 to 2	95 to 100%	0.3	0.28
Onions	3.0	0.9	0.045 to 0.120	-1 to 0	70 to 75%	0.3	0.28
Potatoes	4.0	1.8	0.005 to 0.020	-	-	-	-
Ware	4.0	1.8	-	3 – 5	90 to 95%	0.3	0.28
Canning	4.0	1.8	-	4 to 7	90 to 95%	0.3	0.28
Crisping	4.0	1.8	-	7 to 10	90 to 95%	0.3	0.28
Red beet	3.0	1.5	0.055 to 0.070	1 to 3	95 – 100%	0.3	0.28

Bulk storage

141

4.2.5 Table 64: Long term storage conditions and properties of root and leaf crops

Property	Onions	Red beetroot	Winter white cabbage	Carrots
			Crop	
Bulk density m³/tonne	2.25-2.5	1.38	2.55	1.7-1.84
Loading depth m	3	3	3	3
Suggested storage temperature °C	0*	1-3	0-1	0-1
Suggested storage humidity %RH	70-75	95-100	90-95	95-98
Freezing point °C	-1	-3	-1	-1.4
Respiration heat W/tonne at °C				
0	9	12	9	39
5	15	21	21	51
10	21	33	24	57
15	21	51	39	71
20	24	57	60	98

*Note: Direct harvested onions require a drying and curing period at higher temperature before the storage regime commences.

4.2.6 Table 65: Guidance on the relative suitability of cooling systems for individual crops - Vegetables

Vegetable	Direct Refrig. cooling	Ice Bank cooling	Hydro-cooling	Vacuum cooling
Asparagus	**	**	***	*
Beans – green	*	***	**	*
Brussels sprouts	*	***	*	**
Beetroot	*	***	**	†
Cabbage – leaf	*	***	*	***
Cabbage – head	**	***	†	†
Calabrese	*	***	*	**
Carrots	*	**	***	†
Cauliflower	*	***	*	*
Celery – field	*	**	**	***
Chinese cabbage	*	***	†	**
Courgettes and marrows	**	***	†	†
Leeks	**	***	***	*
Lettuce Butterhead	*	**	†	***
Crisp	*	**	†	***
Onions – dry bulb	***	†	†	†
Onions – salad	*	**	***	**
Parsnips	*	**	***	†
Peas – pod	*	***	**	*
Potatoes – new	**	***	†	†
Radish	*	*	***	†
Rhubarb	*	***	†	*
Sweet corn	*	***	*	**
Watercress	†	*	***	*

Key: *** Most suitable
     ** Suitable
     * Satisfactory
     † Unsuitable

4.2.7 Table 66: Guidance on the relative suitability of cooling systems for individual crops - Fruit

Fruit	Direct Refrig. cooling	Ice Bank cooling	Hydro-cooling	Vacuum cooling
Apples	***	**	*	†
Blackberries	**	***	†	†
Blackcurrants	**	***	†	†
Cherries	***	**	*	†
Gooseberries	**	***	†	†
Pears	***	**	*	†
Plums	***	**	*	†
Raspberries	**	***	†	†
Strawberries	**	***	†	†
Key:	*** Most suitable		** Suitable	
	*Satisfactory		† Unsuitable	

4.2.8 Table 67: Guidance on the relative suitability of cooling systems for individual crops - Protected crops

Protected crops	Direct Refrig. cooling	Ice Bank cooling	Hydro-cooling	Vacuum cooling
Bulb flowers	***	**	†	***
Carnations	**	**	†	***
Celery protected	*	**	†	***
Chinese cabbage	*	***	†	**
Chrysanthemums	**	**	†	***
Cress	**	***	†	***
Cucumber	**	***	*	†
Lettuce Butterhead and Crisp	**	**	*	†
Mushrooms	*	**	†	***
Sweet peppers	**	***	†	†
Tomatoes	**	**	***	†
Key:	*** Most suitable		** Suitable	
	*Satisfactory		† Unsuitable	

4.2.9 Table 68: Typical figures for heat production and volume - Fruit

Crop	Maximum rate of production of heat for a range of temperatures in W/t					Specific heat kJ (kg k)	Volume of crop/bulk m³/t
Fruit	0°C	5°C	10°C	15°C	20°C		
Apples	10	19	30	39	46	3.64	1.90
Blackcurrants	44	77	111	259	272	3.68	-
Cherries	16	47	91	130	160	3.52	2.46
Gooseberries	26	49	75	92	100	3.81	2.05
Pears	11	39	73	110	156	3.60	1.59
Raspberries	69	158	292	389	576	3.56	-
Strawberries	43	80	147	245	374	3.85	2.18
Tomatoes	17	26	43	66	86	3.98	2.44

Key: (b) = Bulk bins, (c) = Cartons, (t) = Trays

4.2.10   Table 69: Typical figures for heat production and volume - Vegetables

Crop Vegetables		Maximum rate of production of heat for a range of temperatures in W/t				Specific heat kJ (kg k)	Volume of crop/bulk m³/t	Volume in store/bulk m³/t
		0°C	5°C			20°C		
Cabbage	White	9	21	2.55	2.55	60	3.94	2.55	4.07(b)
	Jan. King	18	39	-	-	170	3.94	6.30	-
Carrots		39	51	2.63(b	2.63(b	98	3.81	1.70-1.84	2.63(b)
Cauliflower		60	101	2.05	2.05	375	3.89	2.55-4.50	-
Lettuce		48	71	1.59	1.59	238	4.02	4.03-5.68	10.59(c)
Onions		9	15	-	-	24	3.77	1.80-2.83	3.85(b)
Peppers				2.18	2.18			4.88	11.84(c)
Potatoes		18	9	2.44	2.44	18	3.43	1.42-1.59	2.26-2.54b
Red Beetroot		33	42			119	3.78	1.70	2.69

Key: (b) = Bulk bins (c) = Cartons,(t) = Trays

146

4.3 Controlled Atmosphere (CA) Storage

All current construction in the UK for CA storage of fruit and vegetables uses pre-fabricated insulated panels with plastic coated metal facing. CA stores can be built either within a steel framed clad building that can also include packing and grading facilities or they can be built as free standing rooms up to a certain size. The insulation in the panels should be carefully chosen to have high insulation value, good structural strength and with a fire rating to meet the insurance companies latest requirements.

The floor should be concrete with the necessary barriers included to ensure leak tightness. For pear stores and vegetable stores expected to operate at between 1 and 0 deg C the concrete floor should include thermal insulation. Thermal insulation can be used in higher temperature stores to improve operating efficiency.

Because CA stores are sealed the internal pressure of the room will be different to that of the normal atmospheric pressure. The structure should be designed to withstand a pressure difference from inside to outside of at least 245 Pa (25 mm wg). This requires a stronger construction than regular cold stores. The structure should be protected from structural damage caused by pressure differences by the installation of suitable pressure relief valves, typically operating at 175 Pa (18 mm wg).

4.3.1 Achieving leak tight storage

For a CA store to be effective it is essential that the construction is leak tight. There are standard tests for this which should be included in the construction specification. It is unlikely that this specification will be achieved without the use of special insulated and sealed doors that have been designed and made for CA applications.

To achieve the degree of leak tightness needed all panel and floor joints have to be carefully sealed with proprietary sealing materials that have a considerable amount of low temperature flexibility. This is so that the seal integrity can be maintained when the panels move with the normal pressure and temperature changes that occur.

4.3.2 Sizes of controlled atmosphere storage

CA stores vary in size in the UK, generally from 50 to 250 tonnes. The choice of size should be determined by the loading and packing capacity of the business. As a general rule a room should be of a size that is capable of being loaded from the orchard within 2 days and the fruit packed and marketed within 7 days of opening.

Once the total capacity is determined the dimensions should be related to the number of bins needed, the bin size in use and the preferred stacking height. It is important that a CA store is tightly filled for maximum efficiency and good gas control. The CA door dimensions relate to layout of the bins to be loaded. It is common UK practice to have large doors to permit the maximum possible number of bins loaded into the room.

4.3.3 Objective of controlled atmosphere storage

The objective of CA storage is to change the composition of the atmosphere within the store from normal room air at 21% Oxygen and 0.04% CO_2 to an atmosphere over the range of 1 to 10% CO_2 and 1 to 15% Oxygen. A typical storage regime is 1.5% Oxygen and 1% CO_2. The exact values are critical and vary with crop, cultivar, storage time required, fruit mineral analysis and orchard factors. CA storage should not be attempted without expert advice from experienced advisors. It is not normal practice to store mixed loads of fruit varieties in the same store.

4.3.4 Specialist equipment

Specialist equipment is required for measuring the store's atmosphere. It is now normal practice to install automatic equipment to measure and control the required machinery. Equipment is required for removing the CO_2 produced by the fruit's respiration and ventilators to provide small amounts of fresh air to maintain the correct oxygen level. Many store operations also install nitrogen generators for the initial reduction of the room oxygen. All of this equipment is available from specialist suppliers experienced in this application.

4.3.5 Hazards

Controlled atmospheres used for fruit and vegetable storage are incapable of sustaining human life and are therefore hazardous. Locks and warning notices should be provided to prevent entry of any sort into a CA environment before it is fully ventilated with fresh air.

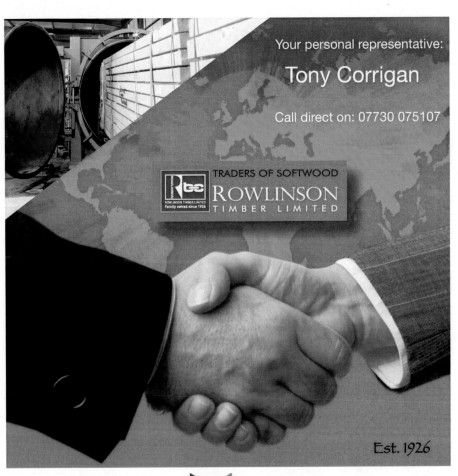

Section 5

OTHER BUILDINGS

5.1 Machinery Storage

5.1.1 Storage sizes

Size will depend on the amount of equipment on the holding.

1. Tractor e.g. CNH T60 80 (155hp)
   4.4m long
   2.6m wide
   3.2m high

2. Tractor e.g. Claas Xerion
   6.6m long
   5.5m wide
   3.7m high

3. Self-propelled forager e.g. Class Jaguar 960
   6.5m long
   3.4m wide
   3.8, high (travel)
   5.7m high (working)

4. Combine harvester e.g. CNH CX8050
   9.1, long
   3.3m wide (without header)
   4.0m high

5. Trailer e.g. 15t payload
   8.2m long (with drawbar)
   2.4m wide
   2.6m (approx) high (with grain sides)

If the implement shed is an extension of the workshop, then it will be Class 1 standard under BS 5502

5.1.2 Access

Site adjoining main access route but set back to allow an 8 to 10m forecourt so that machinery awaiting attention does not obstruct the access road. Due to noise and fire hazard keep well away from livestock and fodder storage.

5.1.3 Security

For security, the more valuable equipment and equipment under repair, may warrant part of a shed being fully enclosed with lockable doors, the remainder may be open fronted. The fully enclosed section needs natural ventilation as for workshop.

5.2 Workshops

Site adjoining main farm access route, away from stock, hay and straw storage, but close to office.

Must have adequate turning space for vehicles, clear of access roads and properly drained wash down area. Workshops are a fire hazard.

Services required are water for cleaning and maintenance needs, hydrants for welding, light and power. Both single and three phase will probably be required. Also step down transformer for hand tools (110 volts).

Security and safety in the building is essential, especially the small tools section.

Small personnel doors for escape should be provided.

Depending on needs and personal preference an inspection pit or lift should be provided in the building, designed to accept any imposed loads from block and tackle gantry.

Size and class usually relate to the number of tractors employed. Building should be Class 1 BS 5502 part 22.

Door openings normally 4.5m high for combines.

Optimum bench size per vice place 2.250m x 750mm x 850mm - 900mm plus 1.500m run for each additional; vice space.

Inspection pit optimum size 1800mm x 750mm x 1700 mm deep.

Wash down area 6m x 6m or 36m minimum.

Lighting- Natural from windows or roof lights on north side (20% of floor area) Electric by means of 10 watts per m2 of floor areas (1/3 of this if fluorescent tubes) plus point lighting at benches and work stations.

Ventilation in form of a protected open ridge outlet. Inlet windows (hopper type) or airbricks.

Drainage by way of a grease/ oil trap to a drain, to meet requirements of the Environment Agency. An area should be set side outside the workshop for scrap metal and waste oil.

5.2.1 Table 70: Workshop details

No. of tractors	4	6	10	12
Employees	3-4	4-5	10-14	14-16
Bench vices	1	1	2	3
Dimensions (m)	4.8x9.6	9.6x9.6	14.4x9.6	28.8x14.4
Bays	1	2	3	6
Optional extras:				
Toilets (m)	2.44x1.2	2.44x1.2	2.44x2.4	2.44x2.44
No. of WC's	1	1	2	2
Mess room (m)			6.0x4.8	6.0x4.8

5.2.2 Table 71: Likely equipment in a workshop

Equipment	Width mm	Length mm	Height mm
Fire resistant welding table	475	950	1000
Air compressor	525	1200	1025
Paraffin cleaning tank	600	750	1200
Mobile battery charger	525	600	975
Pillar drill	400	675	1750
Grinder and stand	525	525	1200
Mobile electric spot welder	525	600	750
Trolley- Oxyacetylene cylinder	750	550	1675

5.3 Fuel Storage

Tanks may be cylindrical or rectangular in section of de-scaled untreated mild steel sheet (black iron) BS 799 - 5:1987, set at a slope of 30-40 mm per m of length, falling away from the outlet.

The tank base to be 1.4m above ground. The tank must provide for 3-4 weeks consumption at 250 to 450 litres per tractor week. If petrol is stored then a licence must be obtained from the local authority.

All installations must comply with The Control of Pollution (Silage, Slurry and Agricultural Fuel Oil) Regulations 1991 - Regulation 5 and Schedule 3 (see diagram.

5.3.1 Open bunded oil tank diagram (Figure 7)

Showing arrangements for both fixed and flexible draw off points

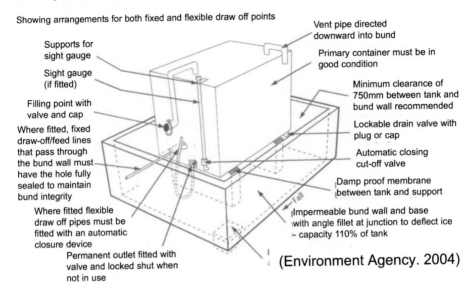

Vent pipe directed downward into bund

Primary container must be in good condition

Supports for sight gauge

Sight gauge (if fitted)

Filling point with valve and cap

Where fitted, fixed draw-off/feed lines that pass through the bund wall must have the hole fully sealed to maintain bund integrity

Where fitted flexible draw off pipes must be fitted with an automatic closure device

Permanent outlet fitted with valve and locked shut when not in use

Minimum clearance of 750mm between tank and bund wall recommended

Lockable drain valve with plug or cap

Automatic closing cut-off valve

Damp proof membrane between tank and support

Impermeable bund wall and base with angle fillet at junction to deflect ice - capacity 110% of tank

(Environment Agency. 2004)

5.3.2 Bunds

- Tanks, drums or other containers must be strong enough to hold the oil without leaking or bursting.
- There must be a 'bund' (or drip tray) to catch any leaks from the container or its pipework and equipment.
- The bund must be large enough to contain 110% of the maximum contents of the oil container.
- The bund base and wall must be impermeable to water and oil. They must be checked reguarly for leaks.
- No rainwater drainage valve may be fitted to the bund.
- It is the responsibility of the property owner to ensure the oil storage installation meets the Regulations and is checked reguarly.

5.4 Chemical Stores

Storage methods must safeguard the health and safety of farm staff and other persons, prevent pollution, safeguard the environment and provide a secure and suitable environment for an expensive commodity.

The store should be dry, well ventilated, secure against vandalism and well lit but avoid direct sunlight.

It should be fire, rodent, chemical and frost resistant. Insulated to U-value=0.6 W/m2K

Doors should be a minimum of 2.1m wide by 2.1m high, opening outwards. Walling should be cavity or equivalent insulated structure with a 30 minute resistance.

Ventilation should achieve 3 air changes per hour, obtained by air bricks at high level or fans.

Natural light from windows at high level in north wall.

Electricity for internal light of 100 lux and external light also.

The floor must be impervious to spillage with a threhold to all door openings. Sub-floor drainage to trapped gully and sealed sump at least 4m from store.

All chemicals to be stored on shelves with a front lip. Empty containers to be stored seperately. Bib-cock with loose union fitted externally within 2m of the door. Block-heat heater at low level with frost-stat to control freezing.

Staff facilities need a room, seperately approached and ventilated with space for clean and soiled clothing, gloves and footwear, wash basin, first aid kit and drench shower. The store should be able to retain leakage or spillage to a volume of 110% of the total quantity of products likely to be stored. Building is the most usual way of achieving this.

The store should be isolated, used soley for chemicals, have a 4m 'moat' space around the store with it being well away from overhead power lines, water courses, ponds, ditches and boreholes. Existing buidlings may be suitable for conversion or it may be new with traditional materials, ready made (prefab) or a secure cabinet. Safety signs must be displayed.

Section 6

BUILDINGS FOR DIVERSIFICATION

6.1 Building/Planning Legislation relevant to diversification

The principal issues relating to diversification are whether it is a reuse of buildings for letting purposes or the application of new or latent skills by a farm or business owner. In the case of re-using buildings, location is a key consideration. Where letting is intended there must be a clear and significant demand for the premises to justify the expenditure, whereas for an owner's own purposes the location can be more secondary as their principal thrust will be as somewhere convenient for them to operate from an which they can provide at a lower cost than taking on a third party's premises in a better location. Grants are hard to come by, so the business plan or investment considerations must be good enough to work without grant; any available grants are a bonus. Costs of conversions tend to be greater than the cost of new build although in many cases a more wholesome result may be possible given excellent attention to detail and quality of finish.

In planning terms it is usually necessary to site the building where it is self-contained and not jostling with other intensive agriculture. The planners may take the opportunity to encourage the removal of less appealing relatively modern structures, and some of these may still be needed, so a cost benefit analysis will be useful.

The main restrictions on criteria for re-use of traditional buildings will relate to limited new openings for doors and windows, limited construction of chimneys and modern "house-like" effects. Some planning authorities are actively encouraging dramatic contemporary design with use of glass and links rather than further additional traditional built sections. The overall requirement is to retain the character of the buildings and their seemingly traditional place in the landscape and for parking to be ancillary and intimate rather than on an exaggerated scale which may diminish the traditional appearance of the end result.

6.2 Farm Shops

The location of farm shops is vital to their success. Planning authorities in some areas are extremely unwilling to see new build, even though Government policy indicates they should be giving consideration to enhancement and encouragement to rural businesses, new or old. The impact of rates must be considered by both the owner/developer and the user. Now rates are chargeable on empty premises it is even more important that a user is identified before the rating authority considers the building to be broadly fit for purpose and usable. It is worth bearing in mind that the rating authorities do keep an eye on planning applications granted and will visit the site.

One of the main difficulties with a farm shop is having a suitable building available for conversion in the right place, which will allow safe access for the users and the continuing operation of any existing farm business adjacent.

The second main major consideration after location will be highways, and there is reluctance in some local authority areas to allow the impact of the farm shop on highways, which can constrain the initial application and certainly any expansion. In certain areas there is grave suspicion about the extent to which the commercial use will expand as they are keen to avoid development of commercial enterprises in rural areas which they consider should remain in urban areas.

6.3 Horses and Stabling

6.3.1 Siting and layout

Usually most convenient in a u shape around an open courtyard. The court yard can face south or south east and be walled and gated to provide control of the animals and security.

The buildings required may include loose boxes, stalls, utility box/ sick box, fodder store, (concentrates, forage, litter), tack room, cleaning, drying, manure storage, office and garage, and possibly covered riding areas and arenas.

6.3.2 Basic and constructional data

The environmental requirements are:-

1. Humidity range 30%-70% RH
2. Ventilation Rate 4 to 6 air changes per hour i.e. 40-45 m3 per animal.
3. For space standards see tables D.1 and D.2
4. Water- Horses usually drink three times per day. Must be clean. Bucket or pressure fed water bowl, both located well off floor. 15mm supply to pressure bowls. 22mm supply to standpipe, serving up to 6-9 boxes.
5. Insulation- See table D.1

Lying area:
      Concrete or cobbles with bedding (straw or shavings).

6.3.3 Table 72: Loose housing in boxes

Occupant	Length	Width/Depth	Eaves height	'U' Value W/m² K	Lighting Level
Pony	3.05 to 3.66	3.05 to 3.66	2.44 to 3.05	0.30	50 lux
Horse	3.66 to 4.88	3.05 to 4.88	3.05	0.30	50 lux
Stallion	4.27	3.66	3.05	0.30	50 lux
Pregnant Mare	4.50 to 4.88	3.66 to 4.00	3.05	0.30 Or better	200 lux
Mare & Foal	3.66 to 4.00	4.00 to 5.00	3.05	0.30	50 lux
Treatment Box	5.50	3.66	3.05	0.30 Or better	200 lux
Isolation box	3.66	3.66	3.05	0.30	50 lux
Sick Animal	4.50	3.66	3.05	0.30 Or better	200 lux

6.3.4 Table 73: Minimum Space requirement

Occupant	Weaned Foal	Yearling	2yr Old Pony	3yr Old	Mare & Foal
Space M²	2.5 to 4.0	4.0 to 6.0	6.0 to 8.0	8.00 to 10.00	15.0

6.3.5 Table 74: Indoor arenas

	Clear dimensions between base of kickboards			Kicking Boards Ht	Angle °	Natural Roof Light % floor area
	Length m²	Span m	Height m Eaves			
Normal	40	20	4.3*	1375 to 1800 min	10°	20% staggered
Olympic	60	30	4.3*	ditto	10°	20%

6.3.6 Tack room

Tack rooms must be very secure and will require high class security furniture, and preferably solidly constructed walling and roof to deter would be thieves. 1 m2 per horse, plus 2 m2circulation. Minimum size 1.8m x 3.6m x 2.4m high. Lighting natural window 1/10th floor area (50% opening) with internal protective grill. Artificial 80 watts fluorescent bulkhead fitting.

6.3.7 Fodder/ Bedding

Normal barn type structure etc. If eaves height is 5m then each m2 holds .83 tonnes. A box used for temporary storage will hold approximately 6.9 tonnes.

6.3.8 Food store:

Usually the size of a standard box- 3.66mx4.88mx2.4m high

6.3.9 Stalls for Livery

3.0 m deep, 1.8 m wide plus manure passage. 2 m double sided layout allow 4 m central passage for mechanical servicing.

6.3.10 American Barn

(Preferred internal dimensions) 30 m x 11 m x 3.66 m to eaves with 4 m central passage with boxes 3.66 m x 3.66 m wide down each side. Two animals per 3.6 m length of building.

6.3.11 Natural Lighting

Roof lights preferably on North facing slope. Artificial light- minimum 50 Lux.

6.3.12 Ventilation

Outlet, protected open ridge and inlet. Hinged shutters inside.

6.3.13 Doors to Buildings

Double leaf 4.5 m high x 3.0 m wide each end with security locking. Doors to boxes - 1.2 m (4.0') wide, located in corner of box.

6.3.14 Divisions

Minimum 2.3 m high of which 1.6 m solid walling and partitions rendered to 1.6 m.

6.3.15 Riding arenas

See Table D.3. Floors to be equestrian sand with rubber, plastic granules on top.

6.3.16 Riding school surfaces and all weather tracks

If the arena is covered and built above ground level then no rainwater drainage is required, other than for roof water and approach areas. General construction is a drainage membrane between oversite soil level and the drainage bed. Membranes can be of Terram, Polyfelt. The drainage bed to be of clean crushed limestone (or equal). Sharp, not rounded, 4o/50 mm, clean and have no fines, Minimum 225 mm deep or greater depending on soil physical characteristics. Organic base surfaces consist of drainage membrane to separate the surface material from the drainage layer. The joints of this material should be stitched or welded to prevent surface material creeping into the drainage layer, also the edges must be returned 200 mm up the inside of the surface retaining boards and fixed with timber battens. Final surface of wood fibre or woodchip 15-30 mm size, or equestrian sand or waxed fibre surfaces. Inorganic base surfaces comprise 40 mm layer of base course macadam laid by contractor, the material should be made of no-fines aggregate, be lightly rolled and have no undulations. Finally, a 150mm layer of equestrian sand with the final topping of granulated PVC or rubber. NB Any sand used must be well or double washed.

6.3.17 Retaining boards

40 mm x minimum 450 high supported at 1.2m centres. The boards must supported at 1m centres. The boards must be 150 mm above the riding surface and set on the membrane or tarmac.

6.3.18 All weather tracks

For all weather tracks the specification is the same as above plus oversite drainage, in the form of 'French drains'. A channel is cut 30 mm wide and excavated to the required depth lined with a drainage membrane and filled with the same 50 mm clean crushed limestone aggregate, used in the main drainage base. A 100 mm slotted plastic pipe may be inserted at the bottom of the channel. The drains are 2.0 m apart along the line of the all weather track and periodically connected to a convenient ditch, or soak away.

6.3.19 Water

Water for animal needs, washing down, sprinklers in riding arenas, fire precautions and the administration block.

6.3.20 Fire hazards

If combining feed/fodder stores in the same 'envelope' as animal housing then attention must be given to the fire hazard. Design must allow for quick release and movement of animals away from the seat of fire.

6.3.21 Electric

Electric light and power must be provided. For lighting see tables D.1 and D.2 on Loose Boxes and Arenas. Pendant and unprotected bulkhead fittings at least 3m above floor level. Cables must be protected in metal conduit. Protected bulkhead fittings 2.1 to 2.4m. Power points of waterproof type 1 per 3 boxes or 1 to 6 stalls. All electrical work to comply with the IEE regulations.

6.3.22 Drainage

Drainage must be to internally sited trapped gullies with sump, thence to foul drains.

6.3.23 Other facilities

Other facilities that should be provided are telephones, an access road routed separately from stock movement and some form of security.

6.3.24 Building regulations

Needs to comply with BS 5950 and depending on length of human occupancy, full building regulations may be required.

6.3.25 Manure storage

Manure storage to be similar to that provided for other classes of livestock. Run off from unprotected manure stores and stables must be collected in sealed underground storage tanks and disposed of in an appropriate manner. Manure should not be burned.

6.3.26 Buildings for riding schools, livery horses and horses/ponies for hire

Buildings will be stabling, feed stores, tack rooms, etc, either in converted or new buildings. There are a wide range of prefabricated stable designs and manufacturers. See section D part 1 above for design and constructional data. Some facilities for grooms can be included, and will require a planning consent (see PPS.7). British Horse Society and/or the Association of British Riding School recommended standards must be observed.

If a riding school is contemplated and riding lessons are given then the premises must be licensed with the local council (Riding Establishments Act).

6.3.27 Rateable riding facilities

All commercial horse riding facilities are 'rateable'.

6.4 A comment about holiday lettings

With many local authorities declining to consider conversion of traditional buildings to full residential, the obvious alternative to commercial development is for holiday purposes. Local authorities have different views on the extent to which a second home qualifies or whether the HMRC guidelines about a maximum length of letting and the period during which the property must be available for third party letting applies. Clearly a letting for a second home will, if located in the right place, have a higher value than a property in need of conversion, furnishing and then managing for holidays.

The viability of conversions for holiday purposes is questionable and depends entirely upon the location and the willingness of the owner to manage the property. During the planning process, the viability of the enterprise may come into question. The applicant may be trying to avoid holiday letting as an option and some local authorities are inclined to think properties for conversion to holiday lets can be converted to a lower standard and therefore cost less than for residential conversion. Experience tends to show that whilst this may be true in some cases, better quality holiday accommodation lets more satisfactorily, more easily and for a higher price than more moth-eaten alternatives, so the cost difference is minimal.

In many areas the standard of holiday lettings is relatively poor, so a range of buildings with good infrastructure and assets such as swimming pools or tennis courts would offer a real marketing advantage and needs to be taken into account when considering the scheme.

Rating should not be ignored. As a commercial venture, rates are based on an assumed occupancy.

In the event of the use of a normal house for commercial purposes, perhaps offices or holiday lettings, a change of consent to commercial may be possible. However it is likely to be extremely difficult to transfer the permission back to a full residential unit later, because o all of the criteria for conversion of business premises to residential will need to be addressed, and in many cases will prove not to be possible.

Section 7

REFERENCES

1. SAC (04/06) IPPC in the Pig and Poultry Sectors. Obtaining your Pollution Prevention and Control Permit.

2. DEFRA (2002) Office of the Deputy Prime Minister. A farmer's guide to the planning system.

3. DEFRA (2009) [Online] Available from:
http://www.defra.gov.uk/farm/working/health-safety/buildings.htm

4. (i) HSE (2008) [Online] Available from:
http://www.hse.gov.uk/noise/regulations.htm
 (ii) http://www.hse.gov.uk/contact/faqs/temperature.htm
 (iii) http://www.hse.gov.uk/agriculture/guidance/index.htm

5. DEFRA (2003) Water, Air & Soil Codes. Summary. PB4029.

6. DEFRA (2003) Sites of Special Scientific Interest. Encouraging positive partnerships.

7. DEFRA (2008) [Online] Available from:
http://www.defra.gov.uk/environment/water/quality/nitrate/nvz.htm

8. DEFRA (2008) [Online] Available from:
http://www.defra.gov.uk/environment/waste/topics/agwaste.htm

9. Statutory Instruments (2008) The Action Programme for Nitrate Vulnerable Zones Regulations. 2008.

10. Marley Eternit (2008) Roofing literature. Personal Communication.

12. Brett Martin (2008) Roofing literature. Personal Communication.

13. Calor (2009) [Online] Available from:
http://lpg-heating.co.uk/lpg-gas-supply/underground-tanks.htm

14. ADAS (2006) Action on Animal Health and Welfare. DEFRA.
15. HSE (2004) Safe Handling & Housing of Cattle.

16. Environment Agency (2004) Pollution Prevention Guidelines: Above

Ground Oil Storage Tanks. PPG2.

17. DEFRA (2003) Code of Recommendations for the Welfare of Livestock. Pigs.

18. Statutory Instruments (2002) [Online] Available from: http://www.opsi.gov.uk/si/si2002/20021646.htm

Section 8

UK Websites for Farm and Rural Building Design

Agricultural (food and forestry):

Web catalogue: www.agrifor.ac.uk- Searchable catalogue of
internet sites

British Potato Council

www.potato.org.uk
Publications by the British Crop Council (BCPC) with a range of
topic related booklets edited by John Gunn e/g/ Drying for disease
control in store.

British Standards Institution

www.bsi-global.com

BS 5502 Buildings and Structures for Agriculture

Part	0:	1992	Introduction
	11:	2005	Guide to regulations and sources of information

Codes of Practice for:

	20:	1990	(96) General design considerations
	21:	1990	(95) Selection and use of construction materials
	22:	2003	Design, construction and loading
	23:	2004	(98) Fire precautions
	25:	1991	Services and facilities
	30:		Control of infestation

Guide to:

	31:	1995	Storage and handling of waste
	32:	1992	(96) Noise attenuation
	33:	1991	(96) Odour pollution

Codes of Practice for:

	40:	2005	(95) Cattle buildings

41:	2005	(96) Sheep buildings and pens
42:	1990	(97) Pig buildings
43:	1990	(96) Poultry buildings
49:	1990	(98) Milking premises
50:	1993	Storage tanks and reception pits for livestock slurry
51:	1991	(95) Slotted, perforated and mesh floors for livestock
52:	1991	(98) Alarm systems, emergency ventilation and smoke ventilation for livestock housing
60:	1992	(98) Buildings for mushrooms
65:	1992	(98) Crop processing buildings (horticultural)
66:	1992	(98) Chitting houses
70:	1991	(98) Ventilated on-floor stores for combinable crops
71:	1992	(98) Ventilated stores for potatoes and onions
72:	1992	(98) Controlled environment stores for vegetables, fruit and flowers
74:	1991	(95) Bins and silos for combinable crops
75:	1993	Forage stores
80:	1990	(96) Workshops, maintenance and inspection facilities
81:	1989	(95) Chemical stores
82:	1997	Amenity buildings

Building Research Establishment: BRE

www.bre.co.uk

www.designadvice.co.uk (free environmental consultation on specific building projects)

Government Agency carrying out/co-ordinating buildings research and consultancy. Huge range of excellent publications

Cadw: Welsh Historic Monuments

www.cadw.wales.gov.uk

Welsh government heritage body

Country Land and Business Association: CLA

www.cla.org.uk
Includes policy and news on current issues

Countryside Agency:

www.countryside.gov.uk

Tel: 0870 120 6466 for order/ publications catalogue, including:
Countryside design summaries. Ref: CCP 502
Design in the countryside. Ref: CCP 418
Rural development and statutory planning. Ref: RDR 15

Dept for Environment, Food and Rural Affairs (DEFRA):

www.defra.gov.uk

Huge website includes ex MAFF

Rural Development Service SW Region for Rural Enterprise
Scheme Grant application for new agricultural business ventures
(including Associated new farm buildings)
Farm Animal Welfare Council (FAWC) also under this site. Detailed
welfare reports especially useful e.g. Dairy Cattle 1997: PB 3426

Publications Catalogue (Tel: 0845 955 6000 quoting relevant PR
reference number

Publications include the following codes of practice/
recommendations:
Sheep 2000 ref: PB 5162
Control of Salmonella 1995 ref: PB 2202
The Water Code. 1998 rev. ref: PB 0585
Pig Welfare Advisory Group Booklets ref: PB 1490 - 1498 inc
Rural Enterprise Scheme: Guidance Notes for Applicants
Parts 1 & 2: PB 5275A & B

English Heritage

www.english-heritage.org.uk

Important website for all heritage aspects inc. listed buildings

Environment Agency

www.environment-agency.gov.uk

Essential point of reference for most environmental issues

Note Water Code etc under DEFRA with PB ref

Health and Safety Executive (HSE)

www.open.gov.uk/hsehome.htm

Tel: Infoline: 0541 545 500

Publications: extensive - to mail order/ catalogue tel: 01787 881 165
   Farmwise 1999 (general guidance) ref: MISC 165
   COSHH in agriculture 1994 ref: A528
   Construction (Design and Management) Regulations 1994
   ref: CIS 39-43inc

Historic Scotland

www.historic-scotland.gov.uk

Government heritage body for Scotland

Home Grown Cereals Authority (HGCA)

www.hqca.com

Publications/ information service or details of their assurance
scheme

National Dairy Farm Assurance Scheme (NDFAS)

www.ndfas.org.uk

Includes complete scheme regulations and checklists.

National Farmers Union (NFU)

www.nfucountryside.org.uk

Support/ publications/ events for members of the NFU or NFU Countryside

Northern Ireland DoE

www.nics.gov.uk

Northern Ireland's gov. dept. responsible for environment, including heritage.

Office of the Deputy Prime Minister

www.odpm.gov.uk

All the latest information regarding Planning Law, Building Regulations etc. Very useful site.

Royal Institution of Chartered Surveyors: RICS

www.rics.org/rural

Main professional body (rural practice faculty) with excellent information service

Royal Institute of British Architects: RIBA

www.architecture.com

Main professional body concerned with building design

Royal Town Planning Institute: RTPI

www.rtpi.org.uk

Main professional body concerned with town and country panning

Rural and Industrial Design and Building Association: RIDBA

www.ridba.org.uk

Most relevant organisation/ journal (Countryside Building)

RSPCA

www.rspca.org.uk

Especially for their Freedom Foods Welfare Standards

Soil Association

www.soilassociation.org.uk

See also organic conversion information service (OCIS) under
www.maff.gov.uk
Standards for Organic Food and Farming July 2000

Scottish Executive

www.gov.uk/what.asp

Includes aspects covered by DEFRA in England

Sustainable Development

www.sustainable-development.gov.uk

The Stationary Office

www.the-stationary-office.co.uk

www.clicktso.com (online bookstore). Privatised part of HMSO

UK Forest products Association (UKFPA)

www.ukfpa.co.uk

Representing UK sawmills. List of members and products.

Water Regulations Advisory Service (WRAS)

www.environment.detr.gov.uk/wwsreqs99/waterfit/index.htm
Water regulations Guide 2000- essential guide to legislation

A short list of some sustainable or 'green' and other useful websites:

Association of Environmentally Conscious Builders (www.aecb.net)

Natural Building Technologies (www.natural-buildings.co.uk)

(www.arc-architects.co.uk)

Cob buildings (www.abbeysmallcombe.com)

Green woodwork (www.borderoak.com)

Forest Stewardship Council (www.fsc-uk.org)

Sheepdrove Organic Farm (www.sheepdrove.com)

Wood for Good Campaign (www.woodforgood.com)

Welsh Timber Forum (www.welshtimberforum.co.uk)

Segal Self Build Trust (www.segal-selfbuild.co.uk)

(www.sciencedirect.com)

The Ecological Building Network (www.ecologicalnetwork.org)

Thatching UK (www.thatc.org)

The Welsh Centre for Traditional and Ecological Building
(www.tymawrlimw.org.uk)

Limetec (www.limetechnology.co.uk)

UK Building Limes Forum (www.buildinglimesforum.org.uk)

UK Hemp Lime Construction Products Association (www.hempline.org.uk)

Construction Resources (www.constructionresources.com)

Green Buildings Store (www.greenbuildingstore.co.uk)

Cornwall Sustainable Building Trust (www.sustainablehousing.org.uk)
Centre for Alternative Technology, Machynlleth, produce a whole range of useful publications etc.

English heritage (www.english-heritage.org.uk)

Historic Environment Local Management (sister site to English Heritage) at
(www.helm.org.uk)

The Planning Portal (www.planningportal.gov.uk)

Communities and Local Government (www.communities.gov.uk) for documents such as PPS7.

(www.direct.gov.uk)

Bibliography

Making the Most of Your Farm Buildings. A guide for farmers and smallholers.- By Langley, R W. (2006) The Crowood Press.

Farm Building Construction
by Maurice M. Barnes & Clive Mander - Farming Press Books and Videos

RIDBA

The Frame & Building Association
www.ridba.org.uk

RIDBA

brings together the common aims of those involved in high quality framed construction, following good practice in safety: with a very wide membership base, representing contractors, designers, colleges, surveyors, planners, manufacturers & clients.

RIDBA

The Frame & Building Association
www.ridba.org.uk

The main aims of RIDBA are:

To promote the interests of RIDBA members.

To encourage good quality design and safety in construction.

To collect and publish information relating to good quality safe construction.

To ensure members' views are taken into account by legislative bodies when preparing new regulations, codes of practice, design guides or standards.

To keep members informed of changes to regulations, standards and legislation.

Some of the ways the above are promoted are listed below

We hold regular Events, through out the UK at both national and regional levels.
Past events have included visits to: The Merlo factory in Italy, JCB, Marley Eternit Ltd, Brett Martin Daylight Systems, Corus Profiles Ltd, Cembrit Blunn Ltd, large steel fabricating factories, innovative and interesting buildings such as the award winning Harper Adams Library.
Seminars on: Part L, health & safety, net rigging, training, retentions, insurance and payment,

We have representation on the following committees: Advisory Committee on Roofwork, NSCC Council and Health and Safety Committee, British Standards Committees B 549 Farm Buildings and B 514 -27 Nets and sheets and the Small Business Trade Association Forum of the HSC

We provide information to members by: Quarterly Journal 'Countryside Building', bi-monthly NSCC Newsline, meetings & seminars through out the UK, construction advice notes, the use of the RIDBA confidential Forum.

We provide opportunities for networking: With other members at meetings, over the phone, socialising, meetings & seminars, etc

As Members of the National Specialist Contractors Council (NSCC) Members have the benifit of: Monthly Newsline, Opportunity for member views to be given to: Construction Industry Advisory Committee, Association of British Insurers, Government, Construction Industry Training Board, Association of Independent Construction Adjudicators, etc.

Members have the benifit of free advice lines on: Health and Safety, Contractual & Legal, Industrial Relations and Tax and Business

Members are promoted by: Being Listed in the searchable data base on the RIDBA website, opportunities for reduced advertising rates, information in members section of our Journal, Annual Members' Directory in our Journal, with Corporate Members listed in centre spread of each issue.

RIDBA
The Frame & Building Association
www.ridba.org.uk

There are three grades of membership, listed below with their Benefits

Corporate Member:

Designed for Businesses

Subscription: **Level 1** for all businesses -   £550.00 plus VAT

Level 2 for businesses with 5 employees or less and colleges -   £175.00 plus VAT

Benefits:

- ✔ Networking with other specialists
- ✔ Quarterly Journal
- ✔ Local and National visits
- ✔ Promotion via the Journal
- ✔ Reduced advertising Rates in the Journal
- ✔ Add your views into **RIDBA's** committee representation to HSE, HSC, BSI, ACR, etc.
- ✔ Print at least one press release in the Journal
- ✔ Up to 4 members of staff can enjoy the benefits of membership
- ✔ **RIDBA** Logo can be used with company name
- ✔ Company name with e-mail and website link in the **RIDBA** website search engine
- ✔ Access to the Ridba confidential Forum,
  - ▸ with advice notes,
  - ▸ information on impending regulation changes
  - ▸ and the opportunity to discuss issues in real time with other members on a confidential basis.

- ✔ Membership of the National Specialist Contractors Council.
- ✔ Free helplines on:
  - ▸ employment,
  - ▸ health and safety,
  - ▸ legal and contractual,
  - ▸ tax and business.
- ✔ Low cost credit checking and credit insurance
- ✔ Low cost Adjudicator nominations
- ✔ Bi-monthly Newsline
- ✔ Low cost retention bonds
- ✔ Training funding for 'qualifying the specialist workforce'

Individual Member

Designed for the Individual

Subscription: -   £55.00 inclusive of VAT

Benefits:

- ✔ Networking with other Specialists
- ✔ Quarterly **RIDBA** Journal
- ✔ Local and National Visits
- ✔ If space allows one press release (if received) will be printed in the **RIDBA** journal
- ✔ **RIDBA** logo can be used with your personal name but not your company name
- ✔ Name in the Ridba website search engine

Concessionary Members

Designed for the student or retired individual

Subscription: -   £30.00 inclusive of VAT

Benefits:

- ✔ Same as Individual Membership

The Frame & Construction Association

www.ridba.org.uk

Membership Application Form
(Includes information for the Membership Register)

Please give your details below in block letters. If you do not want your details to be published please mark a cross here ( )
We/I wish to become members of **RIDBA** and agree to pay the annual subscription on 1 October each year.

Name of Individual, Company or College (as applicable)

Address

Post Code	Tel No	Fax No

Web address	E.mail address

Contact:: - Title Mr./Mrs./Miss.   Initials   Surname

Position

Professional or other qualifications (abbreviations)

Business, please describe materials, products or services offered, If a College please describe courses available.

Please Provide 2 references.	
Name	Name
Address	Address
Phone:	Phone:
Signed	Date

The referees will be contacted by letter and their reply passed to the Membership Sub committee, made up of the Secretary, Chairman, Vice Chairman and Treasurer for consideration. The Prospective Member will be advised of the Sub committees decision as soon as possible. **RIDBA** reserves the right to refuse membership.

The following prices are inclusive of VAT.
Membership (circle), Corporate Business Level 1 - £646.25, Corporate Business Level 2* - £205.63, Individual - £55.00, Concessionary - £30.00. *For all colleges and business with 5 employees or less.
All the above prices are inclusive of VAT

Please return to the National Secretary with your cheque made payable to RIDBA. A VAT receipt will be provided.

National Secretary, Tony Hutchinson
5a The Maltings, Stowupland Road, Stowmarket, Suffolk IP14 5AG
Tel: 01449 676049, Fax: 01449 770028, E-mail: secretary@ridba.org.uk, Web: www.ridba.org.uk

INDEX

Content   Page no

Content   Page no

Content

Page no

Content Page no

Content

Page no

Content

Page no

Content   Page no

Content

Page no

Content   Page no